Hibernian Green on the Silver Screen

Recent Titles in
Contributions to the Study of Popular Culture

HIBERNIAN GREEN
☆ ☆ ON THE
SILVER SCREEN
☆ ☆

The Irish and American Movies

Joseph M. Curran

Contributions to the Study of Popular Culture, Number 23

GREENWOOD PRESS
NEW YORK · WESTPORT, CONNECTICUT · LONDON

Library of Congress Cataloging-in-Publication Data

Curran, Joseph M.
  Hibernian green on the silver screen : the Irish and American
movies / Joseph M. Curran.
    p. cm.—(Contributions to the study of popular culture.
ISSN 0198–9871 ; no. 23)
  Bibliography: p.
  Includes index.
  ISBN 0–313–26491–0 (lib. bdg. : alk. paper)
  1. Irish Americans in the motion picture industry. 2. Irish
Americans in motion pictures. 3. Motion pictures—United States—
History. I. Title. II. Series.
PN1995.9.I67C87   1989
384′.8′089916207—dc19   88–24749

British Library Cataloguing in Publication Data is available.

Library of Congress Catalog Card Number: 88–24749
ISBN: 0–313–26491–0
ISSN: 0198–9871

First published in 1989

Greenwood Press, Inc.
88 Post Road West, Westport, Connecticut   06881

Printed in the United States of America

The paper used in this book complies with the
Permanent Paper Standard issued by the National
Information Standards Organization (Z39.48–1984).
10 9 8 7 6 5 4 3 2 1

Copyright Acknowledgments

The author acknowledges and thanks the following individuals and organizations for their permission to publish copyrighted material:

Dan Ford, for permission to quote extracts from the John Ford Papers.

Lincoln Kirstein, for permission to quote extracts from "James Cagney and the American Hero," originally published in *The Hound & Horn* (April/June, 1932) and reprinted in *American Film Criticism: From the Beginnings to Citizen Kane*, edited by Stanley Kauffmann, with Bruce Henstell, New York: Liveright, 1972.

The Museum of Modern Art/Film Stills Archive for providing the photographs used in this book.

To John and Marietta Blasi,
Who are what everyone should be
But so very few are

☆ ☆ ☆

Contents

☆ ☆ ☆

Illustrations

Illustrations follow page 72.

☆ ☆ ☆

Acknowledgments

For their assistance in my research for this study, I should like to thank the staffs of the:

- Film Study Center, Museum of Modern Art (MOMA), New York City
- Motion Picture, Broadcasting and Recorded Sound Division, Library of Congress, Washington, D.C.
- Film and Manuscripts Archive, Wisconsin Center for Film and Theater Research, Madison, Wisconsin
- Manuscripts Department, Lilly Library, Indiana University, Bloomington, Indiana

I must also acknowledge my indebtedness to *Current Biography* and Ephraim Katz's *Film Encyclopedia,* both of which were indispensable research aids. Professor Lawrence J. McCaffrey of Loyola University, Chicago, gave me the idea for this study. A grant from Le Moyne College's Faculty Research and Development Committee facilitated my work. Professor John W. Langdon and Ms. Joan Mattes of Le Moyne College helped prepare the manuscript for publication. Marietta Blasi did most of the typing; my gratitude to her is best expressed in the book's dedication.

Introduction

For almost three centuries after the first settlement of the English colonies Ireland sent large groups of newcomers to America. In the first half of the 19th century the steady stream of travelers grew into the first of the great mass migrations to the United States. Irish immigrants provided the rapidly expanding nation with an army of unskilled laborers and much of the leadership of the Catholic church, big-city politics, and the labor unions. A decline in immigration from Ireland in the half-century after 1920 has combined with the successful assimilation of earlier arrivals and their descendants into the social mainstream to diminish the effect of the Irish presence on the American scene.[1]

The movies have always been a business, yes, but at the same time they have provided entertainment for countless millions of Americans, and others throughout the world. The movies have also been a mirror, both absorbing and reflecting the society that created it; and while they do not necessarily provide us with an accurate historical portrait of their milieu, they can, with careful analysis, tell us a great deal.[2]

The foregoing statements affirm the importance of Irish Americans and motion pictures in our nation's history. As this study will show, they have had a long and close relationship that has been of great mutual benefit. The Irish not only provided motion pictures with a host of talented performers, but they also contributed to the success of the industry in a number of other ways. The industry reciprocated by making more movies about the Irish than any other ethnic minority. Furthermore, by reflecting and sometimes influencing their audience's changing perception of the Irish, motion pictures facilitated their assimilation into American society, helping to raise both their status and aspirations. In films, as in the nation at large, the pioneers of the urban ghetto blazed the trail for other minorities whose extensive treatment on the screen is of much more recent vintage.

This introductory study surveys and offers some reflections on the symbiosis of the Irish and American movies. As a pioneer effort, it doubtless has its share of shortcomings, but some of them at least were unavoidable. The great majority of silent films no longer exists, having been lost or destroyed, and only a handful about the Irish survives. Moreover, reliable information about the people who made the movies and about other important aspects of the film industry is often difficult or even impossible to find. Whatever the limitations imposed on research, however, the subject is well worth studying, for it represents an important part of the history of American popular culture. Mr. Martin Dooley, Finley Peter Dunne's famous immigrant sage, once remarked that "histhry is a post-mortem examination. It tells ye what a counthry died iv. But I'd like to know what it lived iv."[3] While writing this book, I have tried to keep that thought in mind.

Hibernian Green on the Silver Screen

☆ ☆ ☆ **1**

The Immigrants

THE "SCOTCH-IRISH"

Of the 40 million citizens of the United States who claimed Irish descent in the 1980 census, perhaps as many as 20 million are Roman Catholics.[1] It is this group, very largely the descendants of Irish immigrants since the mid-nineteenth century, that constitutes the subject of this study. Irish Protestants, the so-called Scotch-Irish, are excluded, except for those involved in motion pictures. Although they very probably outnumber Irish Catholics, the Scotch-Irish have been an integral part of the Anglo-Saxon "establishment" in this country for so long that they are not perceived as Irish by society at large, nor are they a self-conscious ethnic minority. Included in my study are those persons who identified themselves as Irish as well as those whom the public identified as such because of their religion or socio-cultural background. This method of selection has inevitably resulted in some arbitrary distinctions where persons of mixed ancestry are involved, but it has not, I believe, caused any serious errors.

From the 1600s to 1845, 1.2 to 1.65 million Irish emigrated to what became the United States of America.[2] The great majority of these migrants were Protestants, mostly from Ireland's northern province of Ulster, whereas Roman Catholics who emigrated were largely absorbed and converted by a host society that was overwhelmingly Protestant in religion and culture.[3] Many of these early immigrants actually were Scotch-Irish, i.e., Ulster Presbyterians of Scots descent whose forefathers had crossed the Irish Sea to settle in Northern Ireland during the seventeenth century, although a considerable number of Anglicans and Quakers also emigrated. Protestants dominated Irish emigration to North America until the 1830s and continued to migrate until 1900, but they were swamped by the flood of Roman Catholics who fled Ireland for the United States during the half-century following the disastrous potato famine of 1845–1849.

Irish immigrants to colonial America were mostly small farmers or indentured servants. A large number of them settled along the frontier from Pennsylvania to Georgia. The "Wild Irish" of the eighteenth and early nineteenth centuries acquired a formidable reputation as fighters and drinkers, but also as preachers and schoolmasters. Theirs was the breed that produced such outstanding political leaders as Andrew Jackson and Woodrow Wilson, as well as Andrew Mellon, the financial titan, and Cyrus McCormick, inventor of the famed reaper. By the 1840s, Irish-American Protestants were successful and respectable members of American society, on the verge of becoming, if not already, a part of the WASP establishment. Thus they reacted defensively to the tidal wave of Irish Catholic immigration that broke over the United States in that decade. As hostile to Catholics and Catholicism as their counterparts in Ireland, Irish-American Protestants joined Anglo-American Protestants in anti-Catholic and anti-"Irish" crusades, playing a leading role in nativist agitation during the latter half of the nineteenth century. To distinguish themselves from the hordes of poverty-stricken papists who swarmed into the cities of the Northeast, Irish Protestants, whatever their origins, began to refer to themselves as Scotch-Irish. This self-description, which symbolized their alliance with the dominant Anglo-Saxons against "foreigners," facilitated Irish Protestants' assimilation into the WASP establishment. By 1900 that assimilation was virtually complete, and today the Scotch-Irish are no longer a recognizable group or subculture.

Although they made up a majority of the Irish-American population, the Scotch-Irish were almost never the Irish portrayed on stage or screen because to others as well as to themselves, they were simply not Irish. That role was reserved for others.

The popular wisdom which regards nearly all Irish Americans as descended from the Catholic peasants who came at the time of the potato famine may be factually incorrect, but in terms of the emotional bonds that created a sense of Irish American peoplehood it is close to the truth. The distinctive characteristics that made the Irish American community unique, and that determined the kind of experience the Irish and their descendants would have in America, were the characteristics of those who emigrated after 1830.[4]

THE IRISH CATHOLICS

The English conquest of Ireland, begun late in the twelfth century, was substantially complete by the end of the seventeenth century. By that time the native Irish had been decimated by savage wars; impoverished by the loss of their lands; demoralized by religious persecution, the erosion of their Gaelic language and culture, and the destruction of their own aristocracy; and reduced to a position that was little better than chattel slavery.

In this disastrous situation, Roman Catholicism became the rallying point for Irish resistance to alien rule and Anglicization. Increasingly it served as the badge of ethnic identity and a repository of native culture for the Gaels. By the time of Ireland's parliamentary union with Great Britain in 1801, restrictions against Irish Catholics had been relaxed, but the country was still governed by an Anglo-Irish Protestant ascendancy, maintained in power by Britain. The mass of Irish Catholics were poverty-stricken peasants, eking out a precarious existence on small plots of land and heavily dependent on potatoes for subsistence. Apart from the consolation of their religion, the one bright spot for these benighted creatures was their family life, which was characterized by emotional warmth and a strong sense of kinship.

It was Daniel O'Connell who undertook the herculean task of rebuilding the morale of his fellow Catholics. With invaluable assistance from the clergy, the "Liberator" created a democratic nationalist movement whose aim was to wring concessions from the

British by means of nonviolent popular pressure. Although O'Connell's mass agitation did win Catholics the right to enter Parliament and hold office in 1829, he failed in subsequent efforts to repeal the union with Britain and establish an autonomous Irish state. Nevertheless, the basic education O'Connell gave his people in the arts of political organization and persuasion was to prove invaluable to them in America as well as Ireland.

The terrible potato famine of 1845–1849, which killed one million people, one-eighth of Ireland's population, triggered a massive and sustained exodus of Catholic peasants. Almost 1.5 million Irish emigrated to the United States in the decade following 1845, and by 1921 another 3 million had followed. This flood of immigrants was unprecedented and surpassed only by the Germans, whose losses to America represented a much smaller percentage of Germany's population.[5]

The enormous influx of Irish (and German) Roman Catholics transformed the position of Catholicism in the United States. In the first U.S. census in 1790, Catholics had constituted less than 1 percent of the population; by 1850 they were 7.5 percent, and by 1860 10 percent and the largest single sect in the country.[6] To native Americans the Irish Catholic immigrants were enemy aliens who threatened the destruction of the homogeneous Anglo-Saxon Protestant society and culture. The dominant WASPs viewed the Irish as a backward and inferior race as well as agents of a religion they equated with tyranny, superstition, and subversion of religious and political liberty. The nativist racial, religious, and class prejudice against the Irish was the product of an English, Puritan heritage, reinforced by a revived Protestant Evangelicalism. To "real Americans," Irish papists were no more compatible with the nation's sense of Protestant Mission or Manifest Destiny than were the Indians or the newly acquired Hispanic Americans of the Southwest.

The Irish became the chief targets of the antiforeign nativist crusade of the 1850s because they were the most numerous and conspicuous Catholic immigrants. The Irish horde swelled the cities of the Northeast, where its members soon became politically active. The Irish insistence on Catholic education for their children underlined their cultural divergence, whereas their support for movements to secure Ireland's independence suggested that their primary allegiance was to Ireland (as well as Rome) rather than to the United States. Highly visible, the newcomers were stigmatized by their strange costume, their accented or limited command of English, their opposition to reform crusades, such as temperance (prohibition of alcohol) and Sabbatarianism, and their frequent drunkenness and disorder. These ignorant, dirty, poverty stricken, and often diseased slum dwellers were a far cry from Thomas Jefferson's self-reliant artisans and yeoman farmers, who served as the national symbols of republican virtue.

Before their movement foundered on the issue of slavery, the nativist "Know Nothings" of the 1850s did their utmost to persecute the Irish and perpetuate the vicious English stereotype of the Celt. At his best, "Paddy" was a happy-go-lucky buffoon, shiftless and tipsy. At his worst, he was a simian-featured barbarian: "childish, emotionally unstable, ignorant, indolent, superstitious, primitive or semi-civilized, dirty, vengeful and violent."[7] His "stage Irish" costume consisted of a ragged tail coat and battered truncated conical hat, knee breeches, coarse stockings, and buckled shoes. Almost invariably, he was armed with a shillelagh, smoked a clay pipe, and was extremely voluble. His hair was often red, as fiery as his temper.[8]

The stereotype is clear enough, and it is part of the truth, for actual ethnic characteristics, however distorted by prejudice, help to create and sustain ethnic stereotypes. But the real Irish immigrant was far more complex than the stereotype, just as reality is always more complex than the oversimplified generalization. To begin with, it is true that Irish Catholic immigrants became and remained urbanites. They settled first in New York, Boston, Philadelphia, and other cities in the Northeast; when they went west, it was to cities like Chicago, St. Paul, Denver, and San Francisco. After the potato famine, the Irish may well have had enough of life on the land; in any case, circumstances kept them from farming in the United States. They lacked the capital, skills, and temperament for large-scale farming on isolated homesteads. A few tried husbandry, but by 1920, 90 percent of Irish Americans lived in cities, with a sizeable proportion of them in large metropolitan areas.[9] In the cities, the immigrants faced the hostility of the ruling classes with neither capital nor job skills. Crammed into tenements in urban ghettos, the Irish found life hard and short, although their high death rate from disease was offset by high fertility. For female immigrants, whose numbers almost equalled those of males, the choice of occupation was simple: domestic service, sweatshop or factory labor (in some stage of textile production), or prostitution, with most choosing the first of these. For the men, it was unskilled, heavy, casual labor—pick-and-shovel jobs that were hard, dirty, and dangerous: digging building foundations, sewers, tunnels, or canals, laying track for the railroads, or working on the docks or in the mines. Those few with money or a trade did better, but not much better in the beginning. Whatever their employment, the Irish played an integral part in the early stages of American industrialization and urbanization. As one newspaper of the time put it: "There are several sorts of power working in the fabric of this Republic—water power, steam power, and Irish power. The last works hardest of all." [10]

To the physical exhaustion, injuries, and epidemic disease that dogged the early post-famine immigrants were added the evils of alcohol. Excessive drinking had been reduced to a relatively minor problem in pre-famine Ireland, but the famine produced socioeconomic conditions that seriously aggravated it. The problem was exported to the United States where it was made worse by the immigrants' terrible living and working conditions and by their partial acceptance of the drunken stereotype imposed on them by the nativists. Whiskey was cheaper in the United States than in Ireland, whereas wages were higher, and whiskey was often forced on Irish workers in partial payment of those wages. For men suffering from cold, fatigue, or sickness, whiskey was a tonic, a restorative. To men desperate and despairing, it offered a temporary escape. Many Irish males (and some females) drank to endure their miserable lot or to forget it. Their hard drinking was noticeable because they were noisy, convivial, and often belligerent. It was excessive drinking that caused much of the crime committed by the Irish—fighting, disturbing the peace, and so on. Their offenses were usually petty and typical of immigrant communities. But drinking and fighting, together with the poverty and squalor that were their cause and effect, made Irish immigrants the shame of the cities, especially in New England where hidebound Puritan Yankees confronted riotous Catholic Celts with no mediators or distractions. In cities with a more flexible, varied, and dynamic structure than Boston or Providence, the Irish fared better, especially in the Far West, where everybody except the Indians was a newcomer. In Denver and San Francisco the Irish became civic leaders, much less given to excessive drinking and riotous behavior. And so it was back East, once succeeding generations of Irish rose higher on the economic ladder. Drinking still remains a problem for the Irish, but one much less serious than it was a century or more ago because of their vastly improved socioeconomic status. Scholarly research has also made clear that the Irish are hardly unique among America's ethnic groups in experiencing problems with alcohol. Like addiction to alcohol, the legendary sexual puritanism of the Irish was primarily the product of socioeconomic conditions following the famine, and it too gradually subsided as the Irish made good in the United States. Although still characteristic of the Irish in Ireland, sexual repression is far less noticeable among today's Irish Americans.[11]

So, as the Yankees stoutly maintained, the Irish did drink, argue, and fight to let off steam; and when pushed too far by Anglo-Irish landlord or American nativist, they pushed back—hard. The Irish were often malicious and vindictive, and they had long memories for real or fancied slights. But they were also honest, humorous, hard-working, and deeply loyal to their religion and their families, which were usually large and almost always centered on the formidable Irish mother, who remains the dominant parent to this day.[12]

With the family, religion served as the sheet anchor of Irish-American life. Catholicism was the proud badge of identity as well as the source of hope and consolation for the immigrants and their children. The church was the center of the local Irish community, and the parish formed the neighborhood. Energetic priests, aided by the "good nuns," sought to guide and uplift the faithful, fighting the public (Protestant) school system, the saloon, and the other forces within and without the Irish ghetto that threatened the welfare of their flock. It was the Irish that made the Catholic church a major part of American life, and for more than a century they have dominated its hierarchy. They created and sustained a unified, Americanized church, overcoming the opposition of non-Irish coreligionists who wanted ethnic churches following traditional European practices. And Irish bishops favored the American principle of separation of church and state, having suffered from the Anglican religious establishment in Ireland. The church also did its best to inculcate patriotism and respect for the law and to encourage self-improvement among its members. In this regard, the church was as "American" as the nativists who feared and hated it. On the other hand, Irish Catholics' stubborn allegiance to Rome constituted a serious challenge to the idea of cultural homogenization and limited Irish accommodation to WASP social and cultural values. Adherence to the faith of their fathers did a great deal for the Irish, but it also cost them a good deal.[13]

Contrary to nativist opinion, the Irish did not take their politics, like their religion, from Rome. Their apprenticeship in Ireland prepared them for active participation in American politics, and they soon became masters of the game. Experience had made them keenly aware that political power meant protection, assistance, and jobs; and they set their sights on winning it from the time of their arrival. Since the Democratic party opened its arms to them, the Irish became and remained loyal Democrats. As their numbers and political expertise grew, they rose steadily in municipal politics. They suffered much abuse because of their power and because of the traditional American prejudice against professional politicians. Although the Irish did not invent machine politics (much less fraud and corruption), they proved extremely adept at it. Irish politicians and their supporters became a principal target of reform crusades organized and led by members of the WASP establishment, crusades not limited to issues of graft and peculation. Whereas many in the Irish community, especially the clergy, supported alcoholic temperance, few supported the temperance crusade, whose ultimate aim was prohibition of alcohol. The Irish also opposed the movement to abolish slavery. They hated free blacks because of their competition in the job market and feared that much worse would befall them if 4 million black slaves were freed. Moreover, they saw the Yankee abolitionists as a fanatical minority willing to break up the Union to achieve its end. Working within the system to inch their way ahead, the Irish had no wish to destroy the Union and every reason to preserve it and promote its expansion, thereby improving their own opportunities. Then, too, the abolitionists, like the temperance and Sabbatarian reformers, were anti-Catholic and anti-Irish nativists—"Know Nothings," "Conscience

Whigs," or "Black Republicans." Unlike their former mentor, Daniel O'Connell, Irish Americans, along with a great many native Americans, turned a blind eye to the evils of slavery. Apart from this issue, however, the Irish were in the vanguard of the struggle for democracy, religious liberty, and social justice in the decades following their entry upon the American political scene.[14]

For those who doubted Irish loyalty to their adopted homeland, the Civil War offered a salutary example of Irish patriotism and courage. Almost 150,000 Irishmen fought for the Union, and the Irish Brigade won renown for its valor. The most famous Irish Catholic warrior was General Philip Henry Sheridan, the dashing cavalry commander who became commander of the United States Army in 1884 and before he died joined Grant and Sherman as one of the first four-star generals in the nation's history. Dedicated service to the Union's cause won the gratitude of native Americans, although Irish laurels were tarnished by the New York City draft riot of 1863. In this outbreak, the worst riot in the nation's history to this day, "Paddy" ran amuck, attacking blacks and denouncing an unfair conscription law that made the conflict "a rich man's war and a poor man's fight." Although this violence demonstrated Irish antipathy to blacks, it had nothing to do with their loyalty to the Union, which remained firm throughout the war.[15]

For some Americans, Irish loyalty was compromised by postwar Irish-American attempts to overthrow British rule in Ireland and Canada. Many Fenians, the name given these militant nationalists, felt that only the winning of Ireland's independence from Britain would give Irish Americans the collective self-esteem and social respectability they wanted so badly. Hatred for England also made up a large part of Irish-American nationalism, but for many Irish Americans, a blow against England was a blow for America as well as Ireland. For such nationalists as these, hatred of Britain and devotion to the cause of Irish freedom were only the other side of the coin of Irish-American patriotism.[16]

Although a large minority of Irish immigrants and their children remained in poverty, the majority substantially improved their lot in the half-century following the Civil War. A higher standard of living, universal primary education, and far-reaching reforms in the Catholic church in Ireland bettered the quality of immigrants to the United States.[17] These immigrants and second-generation

Irish Americans enjoyed greater social mobility than their fore-bears. Replaced as casual, unskilled labor by newer immigrants from Southern and Eastern Europe, Irishmen rose from tracklayers to engineers on the railroads and from millhands to foremen in factories. By 1900, of the 1.2 million Irish males in blue-collar jobs, 930,000 or 75 percent were skilled laborers, most of them working in trades that the Irish themselves had unionized.[18] Although Irish efforts at labor organizing suffered because of the terrorist activities of such groups as the Molly Maguires in the Pennsylvania coal fields, the Irish played a vital role in this area, first as craft-union leaders, then as important figures in the Knights of Labor and the American Federation of Labor. But Irishmen were no longer confined to blue-collar jobs. They also became policemen, firemen, journalists, entertainers, and professional athletes. Graduating from Catholic colleges, some became lawyers, doctors, pharmacists, and engineers. A growing number owned their own businesses, especially in the construction and liquor trades. Although two-thirds of Irish working women remained in unskilled jobs in 1900, an increasing minority were becoming nurses, secretaries, public schoolteachers, and nuns, and fewer Irishwomen were obliged to work as their male relatives achieved upward social mobility.

Between 1870 and 1920, the Irish consolidated their control of the Catholic church and urban politics, serving as mediators between the WASP establishment and the new immigrants from Southern and Eastern Europe. Whatever the shortcomings of Irish machine politicians, they provided essential services to new arrivals and "government with a human face" to the urban masses. Reformers might rant and rage, but Irish machines remained in power because they offered the voters programs more appealing than financial retrenchment and puritanical "blue laws." And however resentful old-stock Americans might be about Irish political bosses and Irish priests, the threat to WASP values and American society posed by "Paddy" and "Bridget" paled in comparison with that represented by the Italians, Poles, and Eastern European Jews who were beginning to pour into the cities of the Northeast and Midwest. As the gap between Irish and WASPs gradually narrowed, however, it became clear that assimilation was a two-way street. Although the Irish adapted themselves to Anglo-American ways and values, they impressed their own particular style on every field in which they were active—religion, politics, labor organization, and entertainment, broadening the course of the cultural mainstream even as they entered it. An obvious example of their impact was seen in the nationalization of the Saint Patrick's Day parades, which by the turn of the century were well on their way to becoming an American institution as well as a celebration of Irish ethnic pride.[19]

The gradual transformation and eventual demise of the "stage Irishman" reflects the progress made by the Irish in the half-century after the Civil War. As depicted in English plays and sketches, the Irish were either blackguards or idiots. In mid-nineteenth-century America, the caricature was less cruel but just as crude, the Irishman being portrayed as less of a menace and more of a clown. Touring the United States in 1837, the popular Irish actor Tyrone Power (great-grandfather of the movie star) played the role to the hilt in the farcical *O'Flannigan and the Fairies*:

Here was the "stage Irishman" in perfect stereotype, dressed in frieze clothes, battered caubeen, and heavy brogans, swinging his shillelagh in a fight at the fair, smoking a foreshortened clay pipe, a heavy drinker, a jollier of the ladies, a believer in the little people, improvident, happy-go-lucky, a buffoon, lacking nothing but a pig tied to a string.[20]

Dion Boucicault (1822–1890), the highly successful Irish dramatist and actor, treated his countrymen more sympathetically. Arriving in the United States in 1853, the prolific Boucicault turned out a string of romantic melodramas that included *The Colleen Bawn*, *Arrah-na-Pogue*, and *The Shaughraun*. His works offer a rosy vision of Ireland, abounding with "blushing colleens, broths of boys, genial parish priests, neatly thatched cottages, carefree songs and dances—all lightly laced with poitin (whiskey) and patriotism."[21] Boucicault's career spanned the transition from the hard times endured by famine immigrants to the more prosperous era of the late nineteenth century, and his portrayal of the Irish reflected and perhaps influenced the measure of acceptance they had won in the United States.

Edward Harrigan (1845–1911), like Boucicault a writer-actor-director-manager, did for Irish Americans what Boucicault had done for the Irish in Ireland. In a series of musical comedies revolving around the activites of an Irish-American social club called the "Mulligan Guard" in the 1870s and 1880s, Harrigan and his partner, the versatile performer Tony Hart, gave an affectionate but realistic portrayal of immigrant life in New York City, with the Irish community in the foreground. William Dean Howells, the doyen of literary critics, observed in 1886: "Mr. Harrigan shows us the streetcleaners and contractors, the grocery men, the shysters, the politicians, the washerwomen, the servant girls, the truckmen, the policemen, the risen Irishman and Irishwoman of contemporary New York."[22] As written and portrayed by Harrigan, the immigrant grocer Dan Mulligan is impulsive, hard-drinking, and irascible, but he is also honest, generous, responsible, and loyal.[23]

Although Harrigan became a theatrical legend in his own time (George M. Cohan wrote the popular tune "H-A-RRI-G-A-N" in his honor), he outlived his popularity. Fast growing in numbers and respectability by the turn of the century, the middle-class, "lace-curtain Irish" were increasingly offended by the "shanty Irish" image in plays and vaudeville sketches, and sought to suppress it. The pressure exerted by the Ancient Order of Hibernians (AOH) and other Irish-American groups eventually brought success in this effort, and by the time the United States entered World War I in 1917, the "stage Irishman" had all but disappeared from American theaters. The fanatical zeal of the AOH in its campaign to sanitize the Irish image was demonstrated forcefully by the Hibernians' boycott of Dublin's famed Abbey Players during their tour of major American cities in 1911–1912. To these hypersensitive guardians of Irish honor and public morality, any criticism of Irish manners or mores was intolerable. Fortunately for theatergoers and those Irish who were not philistines, the AOH Abbey boycotts were a failure.[24] And, with poetic justice, the social pretensions of the "lace-curtain Irish" would be frequently satirized as the new century unfolded in the long-running comic strip "Bringing Up Father" ("Maggie and Jiggs") and in plays and movies like *The Unsinkable Molly Brown*. Perhaps this particular Irish breed was best summed up in comedian Fred Allen's (John Florence Sullivan) acute and hilarious definition: "They have fruit in the house when nobody is sick."

As the "stage Irishman" was being driven from the stage, Irish artists were winning new popularity there. James O'Neill, dramatist Eugene O'Neill's immigrant father, achieved fame and fortune (although not artistic fulfillment) with his long-running portrayal of *The Count of Monte Cristo*. Dublin-born Victor Herbert became a highly successful composer of romatic operettas, including the popular *Eileen*. Fiske O'Hara, Chauncey Olcott, and the magnificent tenor John MacCormack were well known and highly regarded throughout America for their renditions of sentimental Irish ballads. Family song-and-dance acts like the Cohans and the Foys delighted audiences year in and year out. The scion of the former, George M. Cohan (1878–1942) attained phenomenal success in the years before World War I as the most versatile artist in the history of the American theater—songwriter, actor, dancer, playwright, play director, stage director, manager, and producer. Cohan wrote many popular tunes, but he gained enduring fame with superpatriotic flag-waving songs like "Yankee Doodle Boy," "You're a Grand Old Flag," and "Over There." His "110 percent Americanism" was characteristic of Irish Americans, and it helped them win social acceptance on stage and off. Cohan's career represents a landmark in the history of Irish Americans, both because he embodied their patriotic spirit and because in him they reached the peak of success as entertainers on the American stage.[25]

☆ ☆ ☆ **2**

The Silents

THE NICKELODEON ERA, 1895–1915

While the Irish and the WASPs were engaged in coming to terms with each other, motion pictures were born and grew from a novelty to big business. The invention and early development of motion pictures, or "movies," was the work of Thomas A. Edison and his staff of dedicated assistants, working in Edison's invention laboratory in West Orange, New Jersey. Unveiled to the public in New York City in 1894, movies were first exploited as a peep-show novelty, but once Edison realized their commercial potential, he utilized a projector to show films to large audiences. Beginning in 1896, movies were employed as accompaniments to vaudeville shows, and this innovation marks the real birth of an industry and an art form that would acquire undreamed of popularity and influence in the next half-century.

` From New York, movies were taken to other cities and small towns across America by traveling showmen eager for quick profits. The films they exhibited were quite short, usually not more than a minute long; but their depiction of exotic locales, comic turns, and action-packed incidents created a tremendous appetite for movies throughout the nation. Most of the films shown around the turn of the century were supplied by Edison and a few other entrepreneurs, who set up studios to produce them in the New

York City area. After 1900 films began to grow longer, many lasting up to five minutes or so, and the first exchanges were set up to handle the distribution of films from producer to exhibitor. By 1907 there were between 125 and 150 exchanges supplying the "nickelodeons," the name given the converted storefronts that were devoted primarily to showing motion pictures. The first such theater was opened in Pittsburgh in 1905, and by 1910 the "Nickelodeon Era" was in full swing, with 10,000 movie houses located mainly in the working-class districts of major cities. Charging a nickel to see narrative features like Edwin S. Porter's *The Great Train Robbery* (1903), movies that lasted ten to fifteen minutes, the nickelodeons constituted a revolution in popular entertainment. By 1910, with production, distribution, and exhibition all established, the foundations of the motion picture industry had been laid.[1]

In 1908 Edison and his major rivals ended their struggle for control of the movie business by forming the Motion Picture Patents Company (MPPC), an organization of ten companies that, with Eastman Kodak as an ally, sought to create a monopoly. Only member companies were licensed by "the Trust" to produce movies, and only licensed producers could buy Kodak film stock, which was used to make movies. In 1910, to enforce its monopoly, the Trust moved into distribution to prevent use of film exchanges by independent producers. The independents continued to fight back, however, led by exhibitor-distributor William Fox, who went into production himself and brought suit against MPPC, charging it with violation of the Sherman Antitrust Act. In 1917 the courts ruled against the Trust, and it was dissolved. But by that time, competition had effectively destroyed it.

In part, the failure of the Trust was due to the drain of talent to the independents and the occasional cooperation between Trust members and independents. More important, however, was the fact that the independents did more than Trust members to gratify the growing public demand for movie stars and feature films. Well-known and popular performers in films lasting an hour or more proved to be the key to box office success and breaking the power of the Trust. Adolph Zukor, a Hungarian-Jewish immigrant who entered the motion picture business as an exhibitor, exploited the use of stars and pioneered the production of feature films in America. In 1916–1917 he founded the organization that became Paramount Pictures, a corporation that merged production and distribution and dominated the fledgling industry. In 1919 Zukor began acquiring a chain of theaters to show his films, thus completing a process of vertical integration (production-distribution-exhibition) and forcing his competition to follow suit.[2]

The struggle to control the motion picture industry was paralleled by a struggle to control the content of movies. Efforts to censor movies date from the year of their birth—1894. For the next sixty years or so, they proceeded on local, state, and federal levels with varying degrees of success. Initially the campaign was led by middle-class Protestant and women's groups. Chicago was the first city to pass a law establishing censorship of motion pictures in 1907. A number of cities followed, and by 1922 seven states had passed censorship laws. But although they enjoyed considerable success at the state and city levels, the guardians of public morality could not obtain passage of a federal censorship law. That failure was somewhat mitigated, however, by a judicial decision that denied movies the protection of the First Amendment (of the U.S. Constitution). In 1915, in the case of *Mutual Film Corporation v. Ohio*, the United States Supreme Court declared that motion pictures were "a business, pure and simple, originated and conducted for profit . . . not to be regarded . . . as part of the press of the country or the organs of public opinion."[3] That decision determined the legal status of motion pictures until the Supreme Court reversed it in 1952, leaving them subject at all levels to legal restrictions on their content and methods of presentation. As the Nickelodeon Era ended, the battle over censorship was just beginning.[4]

Despite motion picture dependence on immigrant patrons in their formative years, "there were very few films which dealt specifically with the problems of immigrants and ethnic groups."[5] But whereas serious treatments were rare, immigrant and ethnic stereotypes abounded in the Nickelodeon Era. The "stage Irishman" made an easy transition to the screen during the movies' first decade, and the image is preserved in a series of short films, generally a minute or less. In *The Kansas Saloon Smashers,* an Irishman is portrayed as a beer drinker,[6] and in *Fights of Nations* (1907) as a quarrelsome beer drinker. In *Brannigan Sets Off the Blast* (1906), a workman mistakenly explodes a dynamite charge with his sledge-hammer, blowing himself into the air and then falling into the hole he has made. *Casey's Christening* (1905), in which a small dog is prankishly substituted for a baby, ends in a fight that reduces the set to a shambles. *The Finish of Bridget McKeen* (1901) depicts the demise of a doltish woman who starts a fire in her stove with kerosene. In *Murphy's Wake* (1903), the "corpse" miraculously revives to revel at his wake, frightening the mourners into flight. In *Washwoman's Daughter* (1903), what begins as a neighborly visit to a washwoman ends in a fight. *One Round O'Brien* (1912) shows a bum taking on all comers in a boxing ring, with a concealed confederate kayoing the challengers with a mallet. Initially successful, the scheme misfires, and loser O'Brien is left with a sore head after being knocked out with the mallet himself. The "Happy Hooligan" shorts (1901–1903), based on the popular comic-strip character, show the vagabond as a slow-witted, "shanty Irish" type. Other films of the 1900–1910 period generally employed the same low comedy approach.[7]

By 1910, however, the Irishman's image had begun to improve on screen as well as on stage, thanks to the protests of the AOH and allied groups and the efforts of humanitarian reformers. Although many Progressive reformers during this period were nativist advocates of immigration restriction, and others were aloof or indifferent to the problems of immigrant and ethnic groups, an influential minority of Progressives was actively sympathetic and sought to help underprivileged minorities through social work and settlement houses. These reformers campaigned for social welfare legislation and defended the immigrant by applauding the value of the newcomers to American society. Theirs was a "cosmopolitan ideal of American nationality—a version emphasizing cultural accretion rather than racial blending."[8] Allied with these well-meaning WASPs were Irish-American leaders of the Catholic church and the urban political machines who championed the interests of more recent immigrants as well as the Irish, and who, along with prominent Jewish spokespeople, proclaimed the virtues of assimilation.[9] In these circumstances

Progressivism began to appear in the movies' treatment of minority groups in the nation. A genuine effort was exerted to represent most minorities native and foreign, by more human and realistic interpretation instead of the conventional vaudeville comic caricatures. The new attitude was due, no doubt, not only to the generosity of the movie makers but to the fact that the minorities themselves were growing wealthier and more important in community life.[10]

Examples of the more favorable treatment accorded the Irish may be found in the movies of Sidney Olcott (John Alcott, the son of Irish immigrants in Canada), a director who pioneered filmmaking in foreign locations. In eighteen weeks during 1910–1911, Olcott shot seventeen pictures in Ireland. These included several of the most popular plays of Dion Boucicault, such as *The Colleen Bawn* and *Arrah-na-Pogue,* as well as sympathetic accounts of the rebels of 1798, such as *Rory O'More* and *Ireland the Oppressed,* and photoplays of poems by Ireland's "Minstrel Boy," Thomas Moore. In 1914 Olcott returned to Ireland to produce more films. One that has survived is *Bold Emmet, Ireland's Martyr* (3 reels, released by Lubin Company, 1915).

Bold Emmet, starring as well as directed by Olcott, centers on the efforts of Con Daley (Olcott) and Norah Doyle to help the rebel Robert Emmet escape betrayal by an informer and capture by the British. Emmet does escape (although in fact he was captured and hanged by the British after an abortive uprising in Dublin in 1803), whereas Con is sentenced to hang and Norah to penal transportation to Australia for their part in aiding him. However, the two lovers are saved by the Lord Lieutenant's pardon because they had earlier helped a wounded British officer and refused any reward for their service. The film is strongly pro-Irish, but the British are also treated favorably; the wounded officer, Major Kirke, is shown to be a gallant gentleman and the Lord Lieutenant as magnamimous in granting a pardon. Only the informer, Fealy, comes off badly: a contemptible villain last seen being manhandled by an angry mob. Some of the exterior scenes, for example, a rugged seacoast, enhance the film's appeal, and there is plenty of action. The Irish characters in this, as in Olcott's other films, are not simply stereotypes. They are complex human beings, oppressed by unjust rule but heirs to a rich cultural heritage. Olcott's romantic view of history is balanced to some extent by the authentic backgrounds of his movies.[11]

Other surviving feature films of the Nickelodeon Era include *How Molly Malone Made Good* (6 reels, 1915), in which the newly arrived immigrant heroine is offered a job on a New York newspaper if she can secure interviews with ten prominent theatrical personalities in a few days. Overcoming physical obstacles and the machinations of a jealous rival, Molly Malone gets the story and the job. In the course of her adventures, she travels from New York City to Westchester County, to Connecticut, New Jersey, and Long Island by every imaginable conveyance—including an airplane. This burlesque of reporter Nellie Bly's earlier trip around the world in eighty days offers a look at the lifestyles of the rich and famous, moments of adventure, comic bits, and a soupçon of romance, all strung together by a highly contrived and flimsy plot. There is not much about the Irish in it, but it does salute a "greenhorn's" pluck (and luck) and makes her an engaging heroine.

Son of Erin (5 reels, 1916) recounts the adventures of Dennis O'Hara, an immigrant lad from Tipperary who becomes a construction worker for a crooked contractor in league with city hall. Dennis tips off the reform party to the graft and corruption, then helps win the municipal election for the reform ticket. In return for his help, Dennis is made a police captain, fulfilling his original ambition, and he is joined by his sweetheart from Ireland, Kitty O'Grady. Together they settle down in their new home, proud owners of the cow and pig they dreamed of having in Ireland. In this film, the story is thoroughly Irish: immigration, economic opportunity, the alliance of contractors and machine politicians, and the importance of patronage and the police force to the Irish. Again, Irish pluck and luck bring about a happy ending. This theme is, of course, a very familiar one in American films (and history), but it doubtlessly had more relevance for immigrant groups than for WASPs.

There is virtually nothing Irish about the short film *A Sprig of Shamrock* (1 reel, 1915), except the shamrock itself, which serves as a symbol of eternal love for the two principals and helps reunite them after their marriage has gone sour. Still, the national symbol of Ireland could hardly be given more favorable notice than this.[12]

The more positive treatment given the Irish in motion pictures during the second decade of the twentieth century probably owed something to prominent performers, even though these players did not usually appear in Irish roles. Broadway matinee idol Maurice Costello joined Edison in the early 1900s to launch a film career that lasted more than thirty years and included direction as well as acting. J. Warren Kerrigan was strikingly handsome, played heroic leads for almost fifteen years (1910–1924), and retired at the height of his fame when he was only thirty-five years old. Three brothers from County Meath, Tom, Owen, and Matt Moore, began long and rewarding careers during this period, playing romantic heroes. And Bobby Harron, the child of poor immigrants, played leading roles for D. W. Griffith before a tragic accident ended his life at age twenty-six in 1920. Successful Irish directors in the Nickelodeon Era included Tony O'Sullivan, Barry O'Neil, and Francis Ford (John Ford's older brother). Mack Sennett (Michael Sinott), like Olcott the son of Irish immigrants in Canada, entered movies from the stage in 1908 and by 1912 had organized his own production company, Keystone, but his story really belongs to the postnickelodeon period.[13]

By far the most important Irishman in the movie business at this time was Jeremiah J. Kennedy, the head of Biograph Film Company. A self-made consulting engineer who began as a member of a railroad survey team, Kennedy was called in by bankers to liquidate the failing Biograph Company. Instead, he reorganized and revived it, making it Edison's chief competitor. It was Kennedy who negotiated the 1908 Trust agreement with Edison and became the monopoly's chief enforcer, "the steam roller of the Trust." Under Kennedy, Biograph was the most important motion picture company in America. It was there that D. W. Griffith and Mack Sennett learned their trade as directors and that Mary Pickford and the Gish sisters, Lillian and Dorothy, began their screen careers. However, having made his fortune, Kennedy retired, ending his involvement in motion pictures before the Trust was dissolved.[14]

GOING HOLLYWOOD, 1915–1930

The year 1915 may be said to have marked the beginning of a new era in the history of motion pictures. That was the year that D. W. Griffith's masterpiece *The Birth of a Nation* strikingly demonstrated both the artistic and financial potential of the new medium. By that time, too, it was clear that the independents had broken the power of the movie Trust. And by 1915 Los Angeles, or more particularly its suburb of Hollywood, was on its way to becoming the movie capital of the United States and the world. Southern California offered many advantages to filmmakers, among them climate, scenery, and distance from Trust headquarters in New York. The combination of attractions proved unbeatable and irresistible.

During the decade and a half following 1915, the movie industry became firmly established in the Los Angeles area. It was organized into a number of production companies or studios, the largest of which were combined with distribution and exhibition facilities in a system of vertical organization. Although a number of small companies survived, the structure of the industry was oligopolistic, with five big corporations attaining dominance by 1930—Paramount, Metro-Goldwyn-Mayer (MGM), Fox, Warner Bros., and RKO. About $1.5 billion was invested in the movie business by 1926, most of it in theaters, and annual box office receipts were conservatively estimated at $750 million. The nickelodeons had given way to larger and more attractive theaters, which included giant, luxurious movie palaces in all the big cities. Total seating capacity was 18 million, and weekly audience attendance in the United States was 50 million.[15]

The studios and the industry as a whole were run by the "Moguls," a small group of men who were almost all Jews of Eastern European origin, products of the "new immigration" that had begun in the 1880s and crested in the period from 1900 to 1914. Adolph Zukor headed Paramount Pictures and Louis B. Mayer ran Metro-Goldwyn-Mayer (with Marcus Loew, head of MGM's parent company, Loew's Inc.); William Fox and the Warner brothers (Jack, Harry, Albert, and Sam) ran the companies that bore their names. These were not the only Moguls, but they were the most powerful by the late twenties. Jews were very numerous throughout the movie industry, for reasons that are not hard to understand. It was a new industry with tremendous potential, one not dominated by Gentiles and one that promised rich rewards for entrepreneurs who could sell themselves and the product to the public. The Moguls were hustlers on a grand scale, wheeler-dealers with a love of movies and a sense of vision that turned a nickel novelty into a billion-dollar business that manufactured dreams for America and the world.[16]

Although the Moguls were, like all successful businessmen, risk-takers, there were some risks they could not afford to take, once movies became a mass-production industry catering to the taste of millions. Depending on such a large audience, moviemakers had to avoid offending any significant section of it. As the industry expanded, movies tended more and more to reflect the beliefs of the general public, to uphold the conventional wisdom, to portray consensus rather than conflict. Not surprisingly, this powerful new propaganda machine supported the social and political status quo much more often than challenging it with new or unpopular viewpoints.[17]

Despite the Moguls' earnest efforts to please everyone, movies exploiting the modern, more permissive approach to sex as well as the scandalous misbehavior of some inhabitants of the film colony outraged the guardians of public morality. In 1922, after a particularly lurid series of scandals again raised the specter of federal censorship, moviemakers tried to appease their critics by initiating a policy of self-regulation. To polish Hollywood's badly tarnished image, the newly formed Motion Picture Producers and Distributors of America (MPPDA) named as its head a prominent public figure, Will H. Hays. Hays was a former chairman of the Republican party's National Committee, Postmaster-General of the United States, and an elder of the Presbyterian church. With these credentials, he seemed an ideal choice to ward off the threat of federal censorship, and so he proved to be. However, the MPPDA or Hays Office, as it soon came to be called, was unable to improve the moral tone of movies. For all his political acumen and public relations skills, Hays lacked the power to clean up the movies. When the growing frustration of the moralists reached a boiling point in the early 1930s, new demands for censorship triggered a much more serious confrontation between the Moguls and the crusaders for effective regulation.[18]

Technologically, the introduction of sound was the great innovation of the period 1915–1930. Warner Bros. was the pioneer in this development, and the premiere of *The Jazz Singer* in 1927 began a revolution that converted the industry to sound by 1930. The transition was a very costly one, and many independent producers and exibitors were forced out of business. Even the big studios were obliged to seek the aid of bankers to cover the costs of sound, and the end result was to give New York financiers decisive power in the industry.[19]

As the motion picture business grew, so did the part played in it by the Irish. Whereas their role in production and management was minor compared with that of the Jews, there were a few of them who made their mark in this area. One was Winfield R. Sheehan, like Chauncey Olcott and "Wild Bill" Donovan, a native of Buffalo, New York. Beginning as a newpaper reporter, Winnie Sheehan enjoyed a brief but successful career in New York City politics before he went to work for William Fox in 1914. As vice president and general manager of Fox Studios from 1916 until 1935, Sheehan played a leading role in that company's organization and rapid expansion. He also served as production chief, playing an important part in the making of such silent film classics as *What Price Glory* and *Seventh Heaven,* and such early sound features as *In Old Arizona* and *Cavalcade.* After he lost his position as a result of Fox's merger with 20th Century, Sheehan became an independent producer but enjoyed only limited success. He died in July 1945, two months short of his sixty-second birthday.[20] A tough Irishman named Eddie Mannix became studio general manager and chief trouble shooter for Louis B. Mayer at MGM in 1925 and remained manager for thirty years; Billy Grady, a talent agent, became MGM's casting director in the 1930s, a position he also held for many years.[21] Joseph P. Kennedy, a lone-wolf speculator (and the future U.S. president's father) acquired a small production and distribution company in 1926, Film Booking Office (FBO). This move enabled Kennedy to play a key role in a series of mergers that culminated in the formation of Radio-Keith-Orpheum Corporation (RKO), an amalgamation of Radio Corporation of America, FBO, and Keith-Albee-Orpheum theaters. Content with a quick turnover that netted him several millions, Kennedy retired from the Hollywood wars and went back East, returning only briefly in 1936 to act as special consultant to ailing Paramount Pictures.[22]

Easily the most important Irish film executives were Mack Sennett and Hal Roach. Their impact, particularly that of Sennett, as producers and directors is hard to exaggerate. Starting as a performer at Biograph in the D. W. Griffith era, Sennett soon moved to the other side of the camera and learned the art of directing. In 1912 he founded Keystone, a production company specializing in slapstick comedy and famous for the hilarious antics of the "Keystone Kops." Sennett utilized talented comics like the young Charlie Chaplin, a bevy of luscious "Bathing Beauties," and a highly inventive imagination to reach new heights in low comedy. With impeccable timing, Sennett unreeled a rapid succession of sight gags, many of them improvised on the spot and most guaranteed to convulse an audience. The "King of Comedy" produced feature films as well as shorts in the twenties, but he did not long survive the coming of sound. Almost bankrupt, Sennett retired in 1935. Two years later, Hollywood honored him with a special Academy Award "for his lasting contribution to the comedy technique of the screen," a tribute he richly deserved.[23]

Hal Roach started in films as a bit player, learned the business quickly, and soon organized his own company. Like Sennett, he specialized in comedy, but to Roach story and plot were more important than slapstick gags. His more sophisticated brand of comedy, in the hands of such brilliant talents as Stan Laurel and Oliver Hardy, insured its continued popularity in the 1920s and 1930s. In the end, it was television that finished Roach's long and productive career. His legacy includes the best Laurel and Hardy comedies as well as the original "Our Gang" series.[24]

On the technical side of moviemaking, Willis O'Brien achieved outstanding success as a special effects man. In a career that spanned almost fifty years, he is best remembered for his amazing work in the original *King Kong* (1933). Cedric Gibbons, born in Dublin in 1893, won eleven Academy Awards for art direction, a record unequaled in that field or any other. He also designed the "Oscar." John Meehan followed in Gibbons' footsteps, winning three Oscars for art direction in the 1940s and 1950s. C. Gardner Sullivan was the most important Irish-American screenwriter in this period. His early work included scripts for William S. Hart's Westerns, and he ended his career writing screenplays for Cecil B. DeMille's epics in the sound era.

Probably the most famous Irish director of the silent era was Rex Ingram, whose best-known film, *The Four Horsemen of the Apocalypse*, catapulted Rudolph Valentino to stardom in 1921.

Reginald Ingram Montgomery Hitchcock was born in Dublin in 1892, studied at Trinity College, Dublin, emigrated to the United States in 1911, and went into films in 1913. After service in World War I, he joined Metro pictures in 1920 where the huge success of *Four Horsemen* established him as a leading director of romantic dramas. Differences with studio boss Louis B. Mayer led Ingram to abandon Hollywood in 1924 and make movies in France. The advent of sound brought his retirement, and he died in 1950.[25] William Desmond Taylor was another well-known Irish-born director. His unsolved murder in 1922 was one of the scandals that led to the establishment of the Hays Office. Marshall "Mickey" Neilan entered the movie industry as D. W. Griffith's chauffeur in 1911. Becoming a performer, he rose quickly from bits to romantic leads, then decided to try his hand at directing. An instant success while still in his twenties, Neilan's career soon began to suffer from his heavy drinking, and irresponsible behavior all but finished his career before the introduction of sound. The many anecdotes about Neilan's antics make him seem an almost stereotypical Irishman. Like Neilan, John Francis "Jack" Dillon graduated from acting to directing. Dillon turned out a number of successful dramas and comedies in the twenties, but his career was in decline when he died in 1934. John Ford and Raoul Walsh were also active directors in the years from 1915 to 1930, but both men, especially Ford, achieved much greater prominence in the 1930s and 1940s. Undoubtedly the most innovative Irish director of the 1920s was Robert J. Flaherty, whose *Nanook of the North* (1922), a study of Eskimo life, made him the father of documentary filmmaking. Flaherty's Irish documentary *Man of Aran* (1934) was another powerful account of primitive man's struggle against nature, this time the fishermen of the Aran Islands. But documentarists have never done well in the Hollywood dream factory, and Flaherty was no exception.

By all odds, the most popular Irish actor in the silent era was Thomas Meighan. Learning his craft on the stage, Meighan turned to movies and became a leading man by 1913. Starring with Lon Chaney in *The Miracle Man* (1919) and Gloria Swanson in Cecil B. DeMille's *Male and Female* (1919), the forty-year-old actor reached the peak of his career. He remained a star throughout the 1920s, and in *Irish Luck* (1925), a contemporary melodrama filmed partly on location in Ireland, Meighan played a dual role—a New York traffic cop and an Irish aristocrat. The movie was a great success, and Meighan's popularity lasted until his death in 1936. Charles Farrell attained stardom playing the romantic lead in the classic *Seventh Heaven* (1927), but his popularity declined sharply in the mid-1930s, and he soon retired from films to devote his time to the development of the now famous resort community of Palm Springs, California.

George O'Brien, the son of San Francisco's police chief, did very well for himself in the 1920s. He became an overnight sensation when John Ford gave him the lead in the 1924 Western epic *The Iron Horse,* and he went on to play the lead in F. W. Murnau's superb *Sunrise* (1927). During the 1930s O'Brien played Western heroes in roles that fitted his rugged good looks. He ended his career playing strong supporting roles in three of John Ford's post-World War II Westerns, an appropriate finish. Timothy John Fitzgerald McCoy, better known as Tim McCoy, was another Irishman who starred in Westerns. His parents were immigrants from Cos. Kilkenny and Limerick, and his father was a Union army veteran and Fenian, who was wounded in the Fenians' abortive "invasion" of Canada in 1866. McCoy, who served as an Indian agent in Wyoming following his service in World War I, was well versed in Western history. He entered films as technical advisor for *The Covered Wagon* (1923) and remained in Hollywood as a performer until his virtual retirement after World War II.

William Desmond, a Dublin-born actor, went from stage to screen in 1915 and stayed in movies until 1940, achieving the most success in serials during the 1920s and 1930s. The highly popular "Skeets" Gallagher started as a vaudeville song-and-dance man, but he also appeared in fifty feature films and many shorts, generally in supporting roles, between 1923 and 1952. Creighton Hale (Patrick Fitzgerald), a Cork-born stage actor, played leads in silents and character roles in talkies in a career that lasted from 1914 to 1949. Jack Mulhall lasted even longer, from 1913 to 1959, moving like Hale from starring roles to supporting parts. Entering films as a leading man and a director, J. Farrell MacDonald had become a character actor by the early 1920s. He was frequently cast as a Irishman, and by the time he died his face was one of the most familiar in motion pictures. Charlie Murray went from a circus ring to the stage and then into movies. Like MacDonald, he was a favorite choice for Irish roles, playing a character named "Hogan" for Mack Sennett, Pa O'Dare in *Irene,* and Patrick Kelly in *The Cohens and the Kellys* series (1926–1933).

Prominent Irish actresses in the 1910s and 1920s included May McAvoy, who played romantic leads in *Ben Hur* (1926) and *The Jazz Singer* (1927), as well as a troubled immigrant colleen in *Irish Hearts* (1927). Marriage brought her retirement in 1929. Nita Naldi (Anita Donna Dooley) played "vamps" until she retired with the introduction of sound. Phyllis Haver (O'Haver) began her screen career as a Mack Sennett Bathing Beauty but graduated to "vamp" and "gold-digger" roles in the 1920s. Like McAvoy, she left the screen when she was married in 1929. Polly Moran was a hilarious buck-toothed comedienne in a career that lasted almost forty years (1913–1950). Her roles included "Mrs. Murphy" in the highly controversial *The Callahans and the Murphys* (1927) and "Maggie" in *Bringing Up Father* (1928). Sally O'Neil (Virginia Noonan) also appeared in *The Callahans and the Murphys* as well as other Irish movies. A popular star, she was best known for gamin roles until her appeal waned in the mid-1930s. Her sister Molly O'Day (Molly Noonan) also played leads in the late 1920s and early 1930s until overweight forced her retirement.

The most beautiful Irish actress of this period was undoubtedly Dolores Costello, the daughter of one star (Maurice Costello) and wife of another (John Barrymore). As a child, she appeared in her father's films. She became a star at age twenty when a smitten John Barrymore chose her to play opposite him in *The Sea Beast* (1926), a highly romanticized version of Herman Melville's novel *Moby Dick.*[26] Leaving films in 1931 to raise her children, she was professionally inactive until after her divorce from Barrymore in 1935, when she returned to the screen in more mature roles. Her most notable appearance in this phase of her career was as the tragic Isabel Amberson in Orson Welles's mutilated masterpiece *The Magnificient Ambersons* (1942). Soon after making this film, she retired for good and was largely forgotten by the time she died in 1979. Dolores's older sister, Helene, had a fling at stardom in the late 1920s, but her popularity did not last.

Probably the most popular Irish actress during the 1920s was Colleen Moore (Kathleen Morrison), whose mother was Irish.

Moore played the quintessential Jazz Baby in such vehicles as *Flaming Youth* (1923) and *The Perfect Flapper* (1924). But she also played a number of Irish roles in films such as *Come On Over* (1922) and *Irene* (1926). Like Colleen Moore, Mary Pickford was half-Irish, her mother being the child of immigrants from Co. Kerry. But despite this fact and her Roman Catholic upbringing, "America's Sweetheart" was not identified as Irish and did not play Irish parts.

The finest Irish actress whose career began in silents was Alice Brady, the daughter of noted Broadway producer William A. Brady. Having proved her emotive ability on stage, she tried movies, playing first romantic leads and later character parts. Her portrayal of the spirited Irish mother in *In Old Chicago* (1937) (for which she won an Oscar) and of unselfish mother love in *Young Mr. Lincoln* (1939) are definitive characterizations. Her death from cancer in 1939 at age forty-six was a tragic loss.

By far the most famous child star of the 1920s was Jackie Coogan. Discovered by Charlie Chaplin who made him his costar in *The Kid* (1921), the six-year old Coogan achieved overnight acclaim for his portrayal of a lovable waif. His salary soared with his popularity, but both plummeted when he reached adolescence. Like so many other child actors, he was unable to make the transition to adult roles of equal importance. Coogan's film career continued until his death, but his stardom ended before he was fourteen.

The list of Irish performers is doubtless incomplete, for it includes only those who were fairly well known. But the sketches do suggest an important fact. Silent players were often typecast in certain roles—romantic lead, jazz baby, vamp, cowboy hero, comic relief, and so on, but no Irish performer was typecast as Irish or Irish American. J. Farrell MacDonald and Charlie Murray often played Irish roles, but they were not limited to them, and some of the performers mentioned never played Irish parts. In other words, no one made a career out of playing Irish types. This would change in the 1930s.

Unlike German Americans, the Irish were not persecuted after the United States entered World War I in 1917. Indeed, the Irish like most other minorities, benefited from the efforts of the government and motion picture producers to make them rally round the flag.[27] However, the superpatriotism engendered by the government and its supporters sounded the death knell for the cultural pluralism advocated by adanced Progressives and ushered in a decade of reaction and intolerance. First came the "Red scare" of 1919–1920, then Prohibition and immigration restriction, while a revived Ku Klux Klan enrolled millions of members with its outright appeals to nativism and racism. Throughout the 1920s the countryside was arrayed against the cities, calling on WASP America to make a last stand against the inroads of alien races and creeds. The excesses of the nativists coupled with the continuing growth of the cities and urban minorities defeated the intolerant crusaders, but the battle was long and bitter and waged on many fronts, including the motion picture screen.

Fortunately for the Irish, they were no longer the nativists' major enemy. Indeed, "Paddy" and "Bridget" were on the verge of assimilation in the twenties. Most Irish Americans were now second or third generation, Irish immigration having crested well before the turn of the century. By 1920 more and more Irish were moving up into middle-class jobs and middle-class neighborhoods; the Irish had even risen above the national average in college attendance. Except for their stubborn adherence to Catholicism, they seemed largely assimilated. The Anglo-Irish Treaty of 1921 and the subsequent establishment of the Irish Free State in 1922 secured independence for most of Ireland. This resolved the "Irish Question" for the great majority of Irish Americans, who were already fast losing interest in Irish affairs, and "permitted them to accept their full Americanization without guilt."[28]

Pre-eminent in urban politics, the Irish played a decisive role in electing "one of their own" to an unprecedented four terms as governor of New York between 1918 and 1928. The champion of the immigrant urban masses, and especially of the Irish, for so he was widely regarded, was Al Smith, the "Happy Warrior" from New York City's lower East Side.[29] The forces of bigotry could not prevent Smith's nomination for president by the Democratic party in 1928, but they did play an important part in his crushing defeat by WASP Republican Herbert Hoover. Given the Republican party's majority status and the country's prosperity in 1928, Smith was foredoomed to defeat. But the fact that he was Catholic, "wet" (opposed to national prohibition of alcohol), and a product of Tammany Hall's political machine hurt him more than it helped, losing him more votes than it won him. Even though he was badly beaten, however, the "hero of the cities" pointed the way to a victorious future for his party. Smith was the first Democrat to carry the nation's twelve largest cities in a period when America was becoming steadily more urban. The urban voting bloc that he helped bring into being was the most important contributing factor to the twenty years of national Democratic rule that began in 1933 with the presidency of Franklin D. Roosevelt. Smith's career showed how far Irish Catholics had come in the United States and how far they still had to go. He had become a national political figure, but one handicapped by his ethnic origins and even more by his religion.

During the 1920s more than 200 films dealing with ethnic or racial themes were produced in the United States, about 4 percent of the total number of movies made during the decade.[30] The American Film Institute's catalogue for this period lists ninety-one such films about the Irish or Irish Americans, but only a few of these have survived.[31] Although none of the Irish movies can be called truly memorable, some were quite popular in their time. Among these are two survivors: *Peg o' My Heart* (Metro, 1922) and *Irene* (First National, 1926) (MOMA), both based on successful plays and both later remade as sound movies.

Peg o' My Heart is the story of Peg O'Connell, the daughter of a poor Irish peasant and his aristocratic English wife, who dies disowned by her family for marrying beneath her station. A bequest from one of her mother's relatives takes Peg to live with her English relations, the Chichesters. Alienated by their snobbery and pretentiousness, Peg's only consolations are her little dog and a friendly neighbor, who she believes is an ordinary farmer. When Peg discovers that her friend Jerry is really Sir Gerald Adair and that the Chichesters' only interest in her is her inheritance, she returns to Ireland, angry and disillusioned. Jerry follows her, however, and true love "united England and Ireland." Although *Peg* is set during the period of the Irish rebellion of 1916–1921, the O'Connells' militant nationalism has little to do with the plot. Indeed, Ireland has little to do with the plot. Indeed, Ireland has little to do with the plot, which is highly contrived and filled with one-dimensional characters. What partially redeems the film is the radiant presence of Laurette Taylor (Helen Laurette Magdalene Cooney), repeating her stage triumph as Peg. A great actress, the thirty-eight-year-old Taylor magically transforms herself into a high-spirited, warm-hearted girl who just happens to be Irish. Her beauty and talent were rarely displayed to better advantage, and it is a pity that this Broadway idol made only three movies.

Irene starred Colleen Moore as Irene O'Darc, with Charlie Murray and Kate Price as her parents. There is not much Irish about this film either; it's simply another romantic comedy about a poor girl and a rich boy. Colleen Moore with her cute face, bangs, and sprightly manner gives a lively performance as the spunky heroine who becomes a fashion model, whereas Murray and Price provide comic relief as Pa and Ma O'Dare. Both are good-hearted, but Ma is ignorant and vulgar and Pa is a shiftless boozer, engaged in an unending battle of wits with his temperance-minded wife. After the usual series of ups and downs, love conquers all, and Irene is united with her WASP sweetheart, an appropriate ending reflecting Irish progress in social mobility and assimilation.

Other Irish films from this period that have survived the ravages of time and neglect include *Conductor 1492* (Warner Bros., 1923, Private Collection), *Denny from Ireland* (1919, LC), *Come On Over* (Goldwyn pictures, 1922, MOMA), and *Ireland a Nation* (1914, 1921, LC).[32]

Conductor 1492 is a first-rate comedy, fast-paced, full of clever sight gags and funny dialogue titles, and including some nice touches of ethnic humor. Emigrating from Ireland to Loteda (sic), Ohio, Terry O'Toole (Johnny Hines) becomes a streetcar conductor-motorman. In short order, the quick-witted Terry saves the life of the boss's son, thwarts a crooked maneuver to take over the company (heroically rescuing his own father from a burning building in the process), and marries the boss's daughter. Returning to Ireland on his honeymoon, Terry thoughtfully provides the local villagers with a gift from "Ameriky"—boxing gloves, with which they cheerfully start a donnybrook that ends the film. Although Terry has plenty of pluck and luck, he is also well endowed with brains, which he makes good use of in every situation he encounters.

Like *Conductor 1492*, *Denny from Ireland* begins in Erin and then shifts to America, more specifically to Arizona, where Denny has fled to escape arrest for a killing of which he is innocent. Once out West, the stereotypical greenhorn is transformed into the stereotypical cowboy, as Denny discards his clay pipe, homespun jacket, and shillelagh for a ten-gallon hat, woolly chaps, and a six-shooter. After a series of highly improbable mishaps, Denny is reunited with his Irish bride Eileen and becomes a deputy sheriff. This film is neither very funny nor very Irish. Like most other "Irish" films of the period, it employs Irish trimmings to provide plot variation and, hopefully, increase audience appeal.

Come On Over is a more genuine article, helped by a strong cast that includes Colleen Moore as Moyna Killiea and J. Farrell MacDonald and Kate Price as Mike and Delia Morahan. When Moyna's sweetheart Shane emigrates from County Clare to New York, he promises to send for Moyna as soon as he can earn her passage money. In the meantime, Moyna will live with Ma Morahan, while Shane boards with Ma's son Mike and his family in New York City. Good-hearted but unlucky, Shane is unable to keep a job or raise Moyna's fare. Returning to Ireland to see his mother after many years, Mike decides to bring both his mother and Moyna back to New York with him. When Moyna arrives, she mistakenly concludes that Shane loves another girl and runs away. With the help of "New York's finest" she is soon found, however, and she and Shane are reconciled at a grand party thrown by Mike's uptown friends, the Carmodys. Despite a plotline that is sometimes confusing, stereotypical characters, and the use of painted backdrops and process shots for its Irish scenes, there is much to like in *Come On Over*. Mike's reunion with his mother is genuinely moving. Although not always at peace, Mike and Delia's large family is full of life and love, with one son a policeman and the other a priest. And the wealthy Carmodys have not forgotten their roots and show that they can dance a jig as well as the Morahans, their old neighbors from Lisdoonvarna. The film truthfully portrays that strong sense of family and community that marked Irish life. If it patronized the Irish by picturing them as highly excitable and overly sentimental, it also hailed them as kindhearted, honest, and upright. Given the movies' heavy dependence on stereotypes and happy endings, *Come On Over* is not a bad picture of Irish immigrants in the 1920s.

Ireland a Nation is a different kind of movie, a propaganda film "based on historical fact." Produced and released in the United States in 1914, it was re-released with added newsreel footage in 1921. The film's strongly pro-Irish recreation of historical events is coupled with contemporary scenes of "the Troubles" in Ireland and Irish President Eamon de Valera's tour of the United States in 1919–1920. Attention is focused on the heroism of Robert Emmet as he faces execution by the British and the martyrdom of Terence McSwiney, lord mayor of Cork, who died in a British prison in October 1920 after a hunger strike of seventy-four days. Although heavy-handed in its treatment of the subject, the film is fairly effective as propaganda, but how widely it was distributed and what impact it had on American opinion are impossible to say.

Quite obviously, none of the films described here are cinema classics, nor for that matter are the Irish movies directed by John Ford—that most Irish of moviemakers—during the 1920s.[33] However, these examples and the American Film Institute plot summaries do make clear that the Irish were depicted favorably in most films. But not always. One film in particular roused a storm of protest from Irish-American groups—*The Callahans and the Murphys* (1927). In brief, the story concerns two friendly but quarrelsome tenement families who are divided by misunderstanding but reunited once the problem is resolved. As the *New York Times* reviewer demonstrated, however, there was more to the movie than this.

It is all-Irish and, as might be expected, full of fights and broad slapstick. It frankly makes no effort at the surprise style of screen entertainment. It is a smash-bang sort of thing all through, putting such properties as a flower pot, a keg of beer, and a baby to proverbial uses—and, with those who have always liked such, hilarity results.

The cast speaks for itself. Those who have followed stage and screen at all know Marie Dressler and Polly Moran. To them falls most of the work—and they work industriously at their mugging for comic effect and fighting for the fun of the thing. Of course, there is an Irish picnic, which in all cross-word puzzles' definitions is the key for "melee"—and in this respect the picture is nothing if not orthodox.[34]

Not surprisingly, the Ancient Order of Hibernians and other Irish-American societies were offended by *The Callahans and the*

Murphys and several other films that they judged to be "anti-Irish." The New York, New Jersey, and Maryland state chapters of the AOH condemned movies that ridiculed the Irish and supported a campaign to ban such films. As a result of Irish-American protests, the showing of *The Callahans and the Murphys* was cancelled in a number of cities, including Washington, Providence, Bridgeport, Jersey City, Rochester, and Syracuse, and its exhibition in New York City occasioned numerous disturbances in theaters. In Boston the heavily Irish Knights of Columbus forced MGM to make cuts in the movie before it was permitted to open. Faced with widespread protest, MGM did its best to appease Irish wrath, claiming that *The Callahans and the Murphys* had been produced by Eddie Mannix, himself an Irishman, and that no offense to the Irish had been intended by the film. In fact, according to MGM, Mannix had sought the advice of both Catholic and Irish societies in Los Angeles during and even after the film's production and had followed their suggestions. However, as the continuing brouhaha demonstrated, MGM had gone too far, and the effective campaign mounted by the Irish insured that no more films as offensive as *The Callahans and the Murphys* would be produced by MGM or any other major studio.[35]

MGM showed its circumspection with *Bringing Up Father* (1928, produced by W. R. Hearst's Cosmopolitan Pictures but distributed by MGM), a film based on George McManus's popular comic strip, which starred Polly Moran as "Maggie," J. Farrell MacDonald as her husband "Jiggs," and Marie Dressler as Jiggs's sister "Annie Moore" (Syracuse Cinefest, 1987). Although the characterizations and humor in this movie are still broad, the sparring among the protagonists is largely verbal, and there are no donnybrooks or fisticuffs. The snobbish, social-climbing Maggie is necessarily treated unsympathetically for most of the movie, but Jiggs and Annie are affectionately portrayed as good-hearted and unpretentious people—the "salt of the earth." In its subject and style, *Bringing Up Father* is clearly more "respectable" than *The Callahans and the Murphys,* as would be the Irish movies that followed it.

Although the protest aroused by anti-Irish films soon died down, it was important, and not only for its immediate effects. It was the prelude in a minor key to the massive campaign that imposed much greater restrictions on Hollywood in the 1930s, a campaign in which Irish Catholics again played the leading role.

It is hardly surprising that most Irish films of the 1915–1930 period were romantic or ethnic comedies or melodramas, that their themes included prizefighting, horseracing, and social climbing, or that the Irish were very often depicted as policemen. It is significant, however, that a considerable number of these films (twenty-two from 1921 to 1930) have as their subject the relations between Irish and Jews. Although these movies sometimes show rivalry between the two ethnic groups and almost always exploit differences for comic effect, the great majority emphasize eventual understanding and friendship. More often than not, it is the love and marriage of the children, assimilated to American ways, that bring two feuding families together. Such is the case with the most famous example of this subgenre, *Abie's Irish Rose* (1928), first a phenomenally successful play that ran five years on Broadway, then a hit silent movie, then a radio serial, then a sound film, and finally a short-lived television series (*Bridget Loves Bernie*) based on the idea. The popular series of movies about *The Cohens and Kellys* (1926–1933) also made use of this plot device. The marriage of the children is not only employed to bring families together but also to teach the Jews American ways.

According to these films, the easiest way to become Americanized is to marry a Catholic girl, enter into a partnership with an Irishman, or adopt a Gentile baby. These Jewish-Irish romance films reign as the assimilationist films par excellence, castigating old world ways, supporting those who turn from the traditional to the modern, and apotheosizing those who consign custom to the history books in their headlong dash to become true Americans.[36]

These movies "almost always show Irish cultural determinants dominating the Jewish, for the Irish are associated with more appropriately American ways."[37]

Having shown their value as brokers and mediators between the WASPs and other immigrant groups in areas like politics, labor, and religion, the Irish were now enlisted for the same role on the screen—transmitting as well as receiving assimilationist attitudes and values. Despite some setbacks, the 1920s marked a substantial advance for the Irish in reel life as well as real life. During the Depression decade, they would continue to progress under the New Deal, and in the movies the thirties would be their coming of age.

☆ ☆ ☆ **3**

Coming of Age, the 1930s

JAMES CAGNEY AND THE URBAN ANTIHERO

The novelty of sound postponed the Depression for the movies, and weekly attendance reached a historical highpoint of 90 million in 1930.[1] But by 1931 the novelty had worn off, and the following year admissions fell by one-third—to 60 million. Having incurred heavy debts to acquire first-run theaters and convert the industry to sound, motion picture companies were in deep financial trouble, and some went into receivership. However, movies retained a strong hold on the public's affection, and the industry recovered most of its losses in the partial economic recovery initiated by President Roosevelt's New Deal. Although the industry was largely unionized under the New Deal, it retained its oligopolistic structure and much of its authoritarian character.[2]

In the hard years of the early 1930s, with box office receipts plummeting, Hollywood sought desperately to stave off financial ruin by exploiting the appeal of sex and violence. This was the heyday of Mae West and Jean Harlow, suggestive costumes and situations, and sexual double entendre. It was also the heyday of gangster movies, which were ideally suited to sound technology and the mood of the times. Whereas gangster films had gained some popularity in the later 1920s, it took talkies and the Depression to enable them to reach full potential. The wail of sirens, the screech of tires and brakes, and the staccato fire of submachine guns were effects no silent movie could provide. Moreover, the Depression gave gangsters and their antisocial behavior a new legitimacy. With millions unemployed, Prohibition and the moral Puritanism it symbolized had become a bad joke. And in a country filling rapidly with apple stands, breadlines, and soup kitchens, there was widespread discontent with the existing order of things, particularly among urban ethnics, who were fed up with WASP prejudice and hypocrisy.

During the lush era of Coolidge prosperity (1923–1929), profits and dividends had risen far more than wages or salaries. Those on the lower rungs of the economic and social ladder—the great majority of the population—had not shared fully in the benefits of America's much-ballyhooed technological revolution. Given crumbs from the table and told to wait their turn for a larger share of the new wealth, they now witnessed the death of their dreams of material success and an abundance of the good things in life. Increasingly contemptuous of authority and embittered by frustration, the have-nots were sick and tired of the old order, and screen gangsters reflected their anger and resentment. The gangsters were outlaws who would not be pushed around by society. They achieved the success their audience yearned for by breaking the rules imposed on the masses by a greedy, corrupt, and hypocritical WASP elite. The gangsters were Horatio Alger heroes turned inside out; their defiance of authority and the luxuries they enjoyed made them very popular in the early 1930s with all those who were tired of being shoved around and were glad to see some of their own kind shoving back.[3]

Despite the controversy they provoked, gangster films proved of great benefit to the Irish. Unlike the Italians, the Irish were not stigmatized by playing or being depicted as gangsters, partly because they also played or were depicted as policemen or priests in these movies, and partly because they were no longer regarded as much of a threat to American society. Moreover, with the Jews virtually exiled from the screen in the thirties, gangster films helped the Irish gain unchallenged ascendancy as the movies' favorite ethnic minority.[4]

The studio that specialized in dealing with contemporary social issues, including gangsterism, was Warner Bros. Unlike the other

Moguls, the Warners, especially studio head Jack L. Warner, were strong supporters of FDR and the New Deal.[5] Seeking to keep down the cost of filmmaking, Warners found many of its stories in the day's newspaper headlines and utilized on-the-lot (rather than location) shooting, inexpensive sets, and street clothes for costumes. Warners developed a number of big stars in the thirties, but the one who became the most popular and highly paid was the quintessential Irish American—James Cagney.[6]

Born on New York City's Lower East Side in 1899, Jimmy Cagney was a short (5 feet, 8 1/2 inches), feisty, red-haired youth, one of a large family raised mainly, in true Irish fashion, by a strong-willed mother. After trying a number of jobs, young Cagney found success as a "hoofer" or dancer on the stage, a talent he put to good use in several films. Moving to Hollywood in 1930, he got his big break in *The Public Enemy* (1931), a Chicago gangster epic. In this movie Cagney launched his career as a "tough guy" and inaugurated a series of performances that stamped the image of the urban ethnic on popular culture as Al Smith had on politics. More than any other actor, Cagney created the character of the urban antihero and made it as important a symbol in American life as the cowboy, and one much more relevant to the experience of modern America. With his "unmistakable touch of the gutter"[7] and his equally unmistakable Irishness, Cagney defined the American antihero—cocky, streetwise, fast-talking, quick-tempered, and contemptuous of authority.

As Tom Powers in *The Public Enemy,* Cagney played a Chicago slum kid who graduates from juvenile delinquent to adult gangster and bootlegger. Tom lives high, jollies his hopelessly naive mother, ridicules his older brother's efforts to earn an honest living, and shoves a half-grapefruit in the face of his whining moll. When his best pal is killed in a gang war, Tom takes on the opposition single-handedly in a murderous gun battle that leaves him lying badly wounded in a rain-filled gutter. Recovering in the hospital, he is reconciled with his brother, and his redemption seems possible. But it is not to be. His enemies kidnap Tom from the hospital, kill him, and dump his bandaged body on his mother's doorstep. The movie ends with his trussed-up corpse falling through the opened doorway.[8]

Although *The Public Enemy* is fast-paced and action-packed, it is Cagney's performance that made the picture a hit, and him a star. As one critic later described his impact:

Twenty-one years ago James Cagney, playing in his first film,[9] invented a new kind of screen character. In more than fifty subsequent appearances he has polished and complicated it, but the type has remained substantially unchanged. . . . In *Public Enemy* he presented, for the first time, a hero who was callous and evil, while being simultaneously equipped with charm, courage, and a sense of fun. . . . The result was that in one stroke Cagney abolished both the convention of the pure hero and that of approximate equipoise between vice and virtue.[10]

This judgment was not a revelation. Contemporary critics praised Cagney's performance in *The Public Enemy,* and the more perceptive of them realized that he was creating a new movie type: the urban antihero. James Shelley Hamilton, of the *National Board of Review Magazine,* noted in May 1931 of Cagney's portrayal of Tom Powers: "The strongest impression is not that a gangster inevitably gets bumped off, but that there was something likable and courageous about the little rat after all."[11]

In his essay "James Cagney and the American Hero," published in 1932, the editor and critic Lincoln Kirstein wrote:

The strong silent man is the heir of the American pioneer, . . . The origin of the lean, shrewd, lantern-jawed, slow-voiced, rangy, blond American pioneer was in the New England adventurer in the West. The type has become a short, red-headed Irishman, quick to wrath, humorous, articulate in anger, representing not a minority in action, but the action of the American majority—the semiliterate lower middle class.

James Cagney, while he is neither typically strong or silent, does excellently as the latest titleholder of a movie-type which either has become or is derived from a national type. Cagney, in a way, creates his own type. After the creation we can put it in its proper niche in the Hall of Fame of our folk legends. Cagney is mick-Irish. He was trained as a tap dancer. He has had a small experience as a "legitimate" actor. He is the first definitely metropolitan figure to become national, as opposed to the suburban national figure of a few years ago, or of the farmer before that. . . . Cagney may be a dirty little low-life rat, a hoodlum, a small-time racketeer, but when his riddled body is propped against his mother's door, mummied in bandages and flecked with blood, we catch our throats and realize that this is a hero's death.[12]

Five years after Kirstein's essay appeared, the tough-minded film critic of the *New Republic,* Otis Ferguson, wrote his own appraisal, "Cagney: Great Guy," in which he described his subject as follows:

Because through this countrywide medium and in spite of whatever its story was about, this half-pint of East Side Irish somehow managed to be a lot of what a typical American might be, nobody's fool and nobody's clever ape, quick and cocky but not too wise for his own goodness, frankly vulgar in the best sense, with the dignity of the genuine worn as easily as his skin.[13]

In 1939, reviewing *The Roaring Twenties,* Ferguson was still rhapsodizing about Cagney, who was now at the peak of his popularity:

The movies have not produced any Hamlet parts for us, but they have raised a crop of people whose movie legend and cumulative work are almost of that stature. James Cagney is one of them, and it is hard to say what our impression of the total American character would have been without him. He is all crust and speed and snap on the surface, a gutter-fighter with the grace of dancing, a boy who knows all the answers and won't even wait for them, a very fast one. But underneath, the fable: the quick generosity and hidden sweetness, the antifraud straight-as-a-string dealing, the native humor and the reckless drive—everything everybody would like to be, if he had the time sometime. But always this, always: if as a low type he is wrong, you are going to see why. In spite of writers, directors, and decency legions you are going to see the world and what it does to its people through his subtle understanding of it.[14]

In his path-breaking *Rise of the American Film,* Lewis Jacobs endorsed the verdict of Kirstein and Ferguson.

The gangster film introduced into American life a new type of hero, personified in James Cagney. He is tough and aggressive in everything, including lovemaking; danger and sex are his everyday life. Women are not adored by him, but are treated without sentiment and are accepted for what they have to offer. . . . He is a man of shrewdness, a man of action, a tireless talker, an indefatigable fighter—and a simple man of the streets whom anyone might know.[15]

Throughout the thirties, in a succession of films following *Public Enemy,* Cagney popularized and perfected the persona he had created, playing gangsters, prizefighters, cabbies, truck drivers, racing car drivers, aviators, reporters, soldiers, sailors, even G-Men (FBI). As Patsy Gargan, Tom Powers, Joe Greer, Chesty O'Connor, Rocky Sullivan, Eddie Bartlett, Brick Davis, Danny Kenny, and Jerry Plunkett, usually battling mediocre scripts as well as authority, Cagney's cumulative impact was tremendous. The economic recovery induced by the New Deal and the restraints imposed by a strictly enforced production code brought an end to moviemakers' glorification of the antisocial gangster. But Cagney's antihero made a relatively smooth transition to the more optimistic era of the New Deal, which saw a sharp break with outworn traditions and opened wider opportunities for ethnic minorities. And whereas Cagney in the mid- and later 1930s was more often than not on the right side of the law, he remained very much his own man, and there was no essential change in his persona.[16] Whatever role he played, he was, in the words of his close friend and frequent co-star Pat O'Brien, "an image in the American scheme of things; of the Roaring Twenties and the Tepid Thirties, of the dust bowls and the bread lines and gang wars. He is the saga maker of the hard kid who couldn't be pushed too far."[17]

Cagney's finest film in this cycle was *Angels with Dirty Faces* (1938), ostensibly a movie about juvenile delinquency and social rehabilitation. It portrays the efforts of Father Jerry Connolly (Pat O'Brien) to keep a group of New York City slum kids from turning into criminals the way his boyhood pal, Rocky Sullivan (Cagney), had done.[18] Despite the priest's dedication and striving, however, Rocky's "reputation" and magnetic personality make him a much more attractive role model for the youths. To show them that crime doesn't pay and clean up the city, Father Connolly launches a crusade against Rocky and his ilk, which wins widespread support. After killing his double-crossing partners before they can kill the crime-fighting priest (and himself), Rocky is captured, tried, and condemned to death. On death row, Father Jerry pleads with him to play the coward at his execution, thereby destroying his heroic image for Jerry's charges and other impressionable juveniles. Rocky indignantly refuses:

You ask me to pull an act, turn yellow, so those kids'll think I'm no good? You ask me to throw away the only thing I got left; the only thing they haven't been able to take away from me? You want me to give those newspaper sob sisters a chance to say, "Another rat turned yellow"? Nothin' doin'! You're askin' too much! If you wanta help those kids, you gotta figure out some other way.

But when he reaches the electric chair, Rocky suddenly collapses, whining and begging for mercy. Whether real or pretended, his cowardice has the desired effect. The movie ends with Father Jerry leading the boys to church to pray for Rocky's soul, this action symbolizing their redemption from antisocial behavior.

In this movie Cagney gives one of his strongest performances, with the powerful scene in the death house as the harrowing climax. By leaving open the question of whether his fear is faked or genuine, the Cagney myth was preserved while the guardians of public morality were appeased. For his portrayal of Rocky Sullivan, Cagney was nominated for an Academy Award as best actor of 1938. He lost the Oscar to Spencer Tracy, a close personal friend who won for his more edifying performance as Father Flanagan in *Boys Town,* proving once again that crime doesn't pay. However, Cagney did receive the New York Film Critics Award as best actor for *Angels with Dirty Faces.*

Long before *Angels,* Cagney had tired of both the tough guy image and the frenetic pace of picture making at Warner Bros. He became an active leader of the fledgling Screen Actors Guild, and he fought for different and better roles for himself, with his rebellion against the studio resulting in suspensions, litigation, and bad feeling on both sides. Cagney wanted to get away from gangster roles partly because he believed that the hoodlum image cost him other, more important roles. In this he was at least partially right. The producers of *Boys Town* wanted him to play Father Flanagan, but the authorities at Boys Town rejected Cagney because of the roles he had played. The part went to Spencer Tracy, whose screen persona fitted the character better, although in real life Tracy was both an adulterer and an alcoholic, whereas Cagney offscreen was a faithful husband and virtual teetotaler—a quiet, modest, reflective man whose private life was never touched by scandal.

Much the same thing happened when Warner Bros. made *Knute Rockne, All American* in 1940. The studio wanted its biggest star to play the famous Notre Dame football coach, but Rockne's widow and Notre Dame ruled Cagney out, partly because of his identification with gangster roles. Pat O'Brien got the part. Although O'Brien was a heavy drinker, his screen and public image was judged morally superior to that of Cagney, whom he had tried to redeem from his errant ways in a number of films, twice playing a priest to Cagney's knave.[19]

Despite Cagney's rebelliousness, Warners hung on to him because he was too valuable to let go. He was among the top ten performers in box office popularity in 1935 and from 1939 through 1943. His salary rose accordingly, and in 1941 he made $362,500, making him the highest paid actor in the world.[20] By that time he had done a great deal to create the screen persona of the urban antihero and define the image of the urban American, giving both Irish Americans and the idea of ethnicity new stature on the screen and in American life. In 1941 Cagney left the role of Irish antihero behind,[21] but he made a final important contribution to the Americanization of the Irish when he played George M. Cohan in *Yankee Doodle Dandy* (Warner Bros. 1942). As shown in a later chapter, that was a case of the right man for the right film at the right time.

Although Cagney's popularity cannot be gainsaid, it may be objected that too much has been made here of his contribution to the character of the urban antihero. It may be contended that John Garfield, Edward G. Robinson, or Humphrey Bogart deserve as much or more credit than Cagney for this character. Although a case can be made for this point of view, it is not a convincing one. Garfield became the classic youthful antihero, but he did not enter films until 1938, and by that time the basic character had been well defined, principally by Cagney. Robinson might be considered a better choice, since his famous *Little Caesar* (1930) antedated *Public Enemy* by a few months and was the film that launched the rash of gangster talkies. But Robinson disliked gangster roles as much as Cagney and was more successful in escaping them to play historical figures or WASP law enforcers. Robinson also occasionally played conventional villains and comic gangsters, which Cagney did not. Robinson was a fine actor, but he lacked Cagney's insolent charm and ability to ingratiate himself. More importantly, the gangsters he played were Italian or Greek, too dark and alien to be accepted as American types. The Irish were more familiar and convincing as urban types because they were both more numerous and less menacing. Robinson may have been the first gangster star, but Cagney personified the role of urban tough guy.

Humphrey Bogart has become a cult figure in the years since his death in 1957, the definition of the alienated American for many students of film and society. But it should be recalled that Bogart did not create this version of the antihero until the 1940s, when he starred in such films as *High Sierra* (1941), *The Maltese Falcon* (1941), *Casablanca* (1942), and *The Big Sleep* (1946). During the thirties, he played "the conventional villain, cold, implacable, and rotten to the core,"[22] often the second lead to Cagney or Robinson who finished him off handily in the final reel. By the time Bogart changed his persona and became a star, the basic antihero had already been created. Unlike Bogart's version, the prototype was not a WASP and not a loner. He was an ethnic, typically Irish, and had a family, especially a loving mother, a girlfriend, and a close pal or two. In other words, the antihero created by Cagney was a more universal and more human character than the burned-out, existential loner created by Bogart. Of course, times change, and the Bogart persona seemed to suit the mood of postwar America better than that created by Cagney. But Cagney came first, and Bogart and others built on the rebellious and morally ambiguous character he had created.[23]

By the time he went into retirement in 1961, from which he would emerge only briefly in the early 1980s, Cagney's place in motion picture and social history was secure. Shortly after he retired, Nathan Glazer and Daniel Patrick Moynihan said of him in their pioneering study of New York City's racial and ethnic minorities: "When it came to portraying the tough American, up from the streets, the image was repeatedly that of an Irishman. James Cagney (a New Yorker) was the quintessential figure: fists cocked, chin out, back straight, bouncing along on his heels."[24] In 1974 Cagney became the first actor to receive the American

Film Institute's Life Achievement Award for his contributions to motion pictures, an appropriate acknowledgement of his influence on the medium.

When James Cagney died on Easter Sunday, 1986, commentators across the country recalled his accomplishments, while Americans who had grown up or grown old with his movies realized that part of their own lives had passed away with his going. Perhaps the *Los Angeles Times* best summed up his impact: "Cagney's electrifying screen personality, coupled with a Depression-riddled America ready to cheer the kind of anti-heroes he played—men rebelling against a world they did not create—catapulted the pugnacious, fast-talking Irishman into a legendary stature that far surpassed his 30 years of movie making."[25] During his lifetime Cagney was almost certainly the most widely impersonated actor in the world, perhaps even the most widely impersonated human being. This popular tribute reflected the cultural importance of the character he had created, and Cagney impersonations are likely to continue for some time to come.

THE PRODUCTION CODE AND THE LEGION OF DECENCY

Although the heads of the major studios had set up the Motion Picture Producers and Distributors of America, Inc. or Hays Office (as the MPPDA came to be called) in an attempt to ward off federal regulation, the Hays Office proved ineffectual in its efforts to "clean up" the movies because the producers failed to cooperate. Public pressure to make regulation effective continued through the 1920s and resulted in the adoption of a Production Code by the MPPDA in 1930. This action was largely due to the efforts of Rev. Daniel Lord, S. J., who drafted the code, and Martin Quigley, who played the key role in securing its adoption. Lord, who was professor of dramatics at St. Louis University, had served as a religious advisor to Cecil B. DeMille on *King of Kings* (1927), a film dealing with the life of Christ. Although his father was Protestant, Lord's mother was an Irish Catholic, and he was raised in a strongly Irish Catholic environment. Martin Quigley was editor and publisher of the *Motion Picture Herald,* a leading trade paper. A fervid Catholic, he was outraged at what he deemed the movies' sexual license.

The Production Code was a statement of Catholic moral philosophy rather than a list of specific prohibitions and restrictions regarding material to be presented on the screen, but the implications of its logic were clear enough in terms of ethics and general standards of good taste. Despite its endorsement by the MPPDA, however, the code was not enforced in the years immediately following its adoption. Suffering heavy financial losses and facing bankruptcy in the worsening economic slump, the producers felt that they could not afford to abandon sensationalism in their films; in fact, they exploited sensational subjects and themes more than ever to bring patrons back to the theaters. Sex and violence were the order of the day, with gangster films the leading offender for including both. Protests mounted across the nation, from religious, educational, and women's groups as well as state and local censor boards.

In the end it was the Catholic church that brought producers to heel, forcing the MPPDA to accept an amended and amplified Production Code as binding and to set up a Production Code Administration (PCA) to enforce its provisions. In this action, Irish Catholics again played the leading role. A small group of Irish Catholic clergy and laypeople who were deeply concerned about the movies' sensational portrayal of crime and vice secured the backing of the predominantly Irish Catholic hierarchy for their campaign to impose effective regulation on the movie industry. In November 1933 the national conference of Catholic bishops condemned immorality in movies, demanded a clean up, and approved the formation of an episcopal committee to plan and implement reform. The eventual result of this committee's work was the creation of a National Legion of Decency in 1934 whose primary aim was to mobilize public opinion against objectionable motion pictures and enforce its will through the threat of economic boycott. The Legion of Decency established a rating system, which every week classified new films as "morally unobjectionable" for all or for adults (A-I, A-II), "objectionable in part" (B), or "condemned" (C). The Legion's lists were published and widely distributed, and once every year Catholic churchgoers were asked to pledge their support for its work. At the height of the Legion's crusade, it had as many as 11 million supporters.

The threat of a mass boycott of objectionable films and theaters that showed them was well timed. Faced with potential loss of revenue from such a large group of patrons at a time of economic crisis, the producers, distributors, and exhibitors quickly fell into line. The Production Code was revised and amplified to clarify it and make it more stringent, and in July 1934 the Production Code Administration (PCA) was appointed to enforce its provisions.[26] The PCA was to review all scripts and prints of every film produced, distributed, or exhibited by member companies of the MPPDA, which pledged not to distribute or exhibit any film not bearing the PCA's Seal of Approval. Appeal of the PCA's decision on any film was narrowly restricted (and rare), and any member who violated the PCA's ruling was subject to a $25,000 fine.

The provisions of the code and the PCA's interpretation of them were much stricter in matters involving sex then they were regarding violence, since sexual license was the primary concern of the puritanical moralists. Although the code banned ethnic slurs and ridicule of religion, sexual immorality and objectionable language—anything that bordered on obscenity or blasphemy—were its major preoccupations from beginning to end. Supported by the Legion of Decency (to which the major studios regularly submitted their films and sometimes even their scripts for approval), the PCA proved highly effective. By 1937 it reviewed and approved approximately 98 percent of all pictures exhibited in the United States that year.

To head the PCA, Will Hays and the MPPDA picked Joseph I. Breen, a former newspaperman who had moved into the movie business by serving as Martin Quigley's assistant in code affairs. Breen and Quigley were the Catholic laymen who had played a key role in the campaign that brought about the formation of the Legion of Decency. Now Breen was to head the enforcement agency that constituted the industry's response to the Legion's crusade against objectionable movies, an indication of how eager the MPPDA was to appease its critics. Breen would remain with the PCA until 1954.

Although there was scattered opposition to the Legion of Decency's imposition of "Catholic" standards on the general public, it was minimal in the 1930s, which saw educational and fraternal as well as Protestant and Jewish organizations rally to the Legion's support. After all, it was the Legion that had forced Hollywood to make the Production Code effective, and it had done a great deal to decontaminate the content of motion pictures by consulting with the studios and the PCA. Through the Legion, the Catholic church had established a kind of indirect control over the movie industry, achieving in one year what Protestant moralists had sought unsuccessfully for almost forty years. Yet WASP moralists and Jewish Moguls had no real cause to complain at this turn of affairs. The WASPs won a ringing endorsement of the status quo by the PCA and the Legion, a vindication of fundamental American values during a critical transition period in the nation's history. As for the Moguls, they were largely content with the self-regulation imposed on them. In the long run, toning down sex and violence was good for business; it saved the studios from a ruinous competition in sensationalism. And affirming the value of social unity, religion and morality, capitalism, individual liberty, and good neighborliness made the Moguls appear as champions of assimilation and conformity, that is, of Americanism.

Thus the regulation forced on the motion picture industry had both good and bad results. It cleaned up movies and made the family film the standard form of feature entertainment for more than two decades. On the other hand, this form of censorship made it virtually impossible to deal realistically with any controversial subject—political or social as well as sexual or religious. Such subjects were generally avoided because they were considered "too touchy," "too hot to handle." When they were dealt with, the treatment was usually superficial and misleading rather than probing and honest. The promotion of mainstream cultural values and social conformity did have some value in a heterogeneous nation, but it suppressed creativity as well as sensationalism. As the liberal Catholic magazine *Commonweal* said of the Production Code: "Some of the provisions are good; some are indifferent; some are anachronistic; some are stupid; and some are practically vicious."[27]

The subject of film censorship in the 1930s is given some attention here because of the decisive role played in the matter by Irish Catholics. To a large extent, Quigley, Breen, and their clerical allies were responsible for both the Production Code and its enforcement. Their influence on movies for the next two decades was therefore almost as great as that of the Moguls who made the movies and much greater than that of the performers who starred in them. That influence was highly conservative, reflecting the reverence of these Irish moralists for both fundamental American and Catholic values and their determination to show that these were compatible.

ROLES, PERFORMERS, AND PICTURES

Among the changes brought about by the more moralistic approach to picture making in the latter half of the 1930s was the introduction of the Irish priest as a major screen character. Although not as original a persona as the urban antihero, he was equally important, perhaps even more so, in his impact on the audience. By defending the downtrodden and outcast, while at the same time upholding the law and basic social values, the Irish priest both reflected and confirmed the public perception of the Irish as mediators between old-stock Americans and ethnic minorities. A much more popular figure than the stereotyped Irish politician, the priest transmitted assimilationist values to the Irish and other minorities, helping to bridge the gap between old and new Americans. As an authority figure, he towered over the movies' usually dim-witted Irish cops. As tough as they, the priest was also intelligent, compassionate, and "streetwise," a man who could be hard hitting (literally as well as figuratively), but one who was not afraid to show his feelings and whose life was dedicated to helping the unfortunate. As a counterweight to the Irish gangster, he more than balanced the social and ethnic scales in Ireland's favor.

As movie priests of the thirties, Pat O'Brien (1899–1983) and Spencer Tracy (1900–1967) defined the character and opened the door for all those who followed them. Although O'Brien's most famous role was that of Knute Rockne, the great Norwegian-American football coach, he was widely known as the "movies' Irishman," a fact duly noted in his obituary.[28] O'Brien had Irish looks and Irish charm, and he took great pride in the heritage on which he capitalized. He played a priest four times in his career, most notably in two movies he made with James Cagney—*Angels with Dirty Faces* (1938) and *The Fighting 69th* (1940), both for Warner Bros.

In the latter film, O'Brien played Father Francis Duffy, the heroic chaplain of New York's famous Irish regiment in World War I, whose efforts to redeem a cowardly malingerer (Cagney) finally succeed, leading the coward to die a hero's death on the battlefield. The already discussed *Angels with Dirty Faces* is a better and more important picture. Although Cagney has the meatier role as the gangster, Rocky Sullivan, it is O'Brien's Father Jerry Connolly who finally wins the struggle for the souls of the youthful delinquents in the film. However attractive Cagney makes Rocky, he is a doomed anarchist. Father Jerry lacks Rocky's charisma, but he is a useful servant of society as well as his church because he has the right values. Rejecting an offer of "dirty money" from Rocky for construction of a youth center, the priest declares that he doesn't want to build the center on "rotten foundations." Inside the center, he concedes, the boys would be clean, but outside they would be surrounded by corruption, crime, and criminals, Rocky included.

Criminals on all sides for my boys to look up to and revere and respect and admire and imitate. What earthly good is it for me to teach that honesty is the best policy when all around they see that dishonesty is the better policy? The hoodlum and the gangster is looked up to with the same respect as the successful businessman or the popular hero. You and the Fraziers and the Keefers and all of the rest of those rotten politicians you've got in the palm of your hand. Yes, and you've got my boys, too. Whatever I teach them, you, you show me up. You show them the easiest way, the quickest way is with a racket or a gun.

Jerry had thought he could solve his problems "from the bottom up," but now he realizes he must start "from the top down," by going after the kingpins of crime and corruption, including Rocky. As Jerry's crusade gathers momentum, Laury (Ann Sheridan) pleads with him to stop "hounding Rocky." Sadly but firmly, the priest refuses.

Yes, Laury, we both love him. I've loved him since we were kids six years old. We've worked together, fought together, stole together. Oh, I'm not blaming Rocky for what he is today. But for the grace of God, there walk

I. I'd do anything for him, Laury. Anything in the world to help him. I'd give my life if I thought it'd do any good. But it wouldn't. You see, Laury, there's all those other kids, hundreds of them, in the streets and bad environment, whom I don't want to see grow up like Rocky did. I can't sacrifice them for Rocky. You see, Laury, they have lives too. I can't throw them away. I can't.

Like other so-called social problem films of the 1930s, *Angels with Dirty Faces* does not really come to grips with its subject—slums as a breeding ground for delinquents and criminals. But it does show the priest on the side of social justice and law enforcement, and in the thick of the battle.

O'Brien made two more movies in which he played a priest: *Fighting Father Dunne* (1948), the story of a real priest's fight to help abused St. Louis newsboys just after the turn of the century, and *The Fireball* (1950), in which, as kindly Father O'Hara, he tries to help a misguided youth, played by Mickey Rooney. Neither film was as popular as his earlier efforts in Holy Orders, but each testified to the durability of O'Brien's priest persona.

Although Spencer Tracy got more mileage out of his portrayals as an Irish priest, he was never identified with that role (or any Irish role) to the extent that O'Brien was.[29] Tracy's talent was such that he could play almost any part—and did. This moody, self-destructive alcoholic,[30] who turned to the stage after youthful service in World War I, became a superb movie actor, whose natural and restrained performances made him the "Prince of Underplayers." Laurence Olivier said of Tracy: "I've learned more about acting from watching Tracy than in any other way. He has great truth in everything he does."[31] John Ford recalled, "He was a great actor—the greatest, I guess, in my time."[32] Tracy won Academy Awards for playing an Irish priest in *Boys Town* (1938) and a Portuguese fisherman in *Captain Courageous* (1937), and he was nominated on seven other occasions for a variety of roles.

As with almost all his other roles, Tracy did a brilliant job as a priest, even though, as a Catholic, he at first worried about playing such a part, given his less than exemplary personal life. In his first clerical role, as Father Tim Mullin in *San Francisco* (1936), Tracy was an unqualified hit. His wisdom and rocklike integrity made him more than a match for "Blackie" Norton (Clark Gable), a boyhood pal who had become the "King of the Barbary Coast." With the aid of a good woman (Jeanette MacDonald) and an earthquake (the 1906 disaster), the priest redeemed the prodigal—winning another victory for God and society, as well as the first Oscar nomination for Tracy, whose warmth and humanity in the role endeared him to audience and critic alike.[33]

San Francisco was a warmup for *Boys Town,* the story of Father Edward Flanagan and the institution outside Omaha he founded for homeless boys. *Boys Town* begins where *Angels with Dirty Faces* ends—on death row—with Father Flanagan listening to a condemned man who tells him that it's too late to help a man whom society has ignored or abused as a child (as Cagney's Rocky Sullivan had been abused). The priest heeds the message, returns to Omaha, and begins work on a campaign that made Boys Town a world-famous reality. Of Tracy's acting, Otis Ferguson commented: "So here he is as the kindly priest but nobody's football, redeeming what is in danger of becoming sentimental or silly by standing through it as simply natural as a tree. For all his homely face and lack of surface charm, he is about the finest figure of a man you'll meet, and I'm happy that he has finally got a part to show it off."[34] With Tracy winning the Oscar for *Boys Town,* he and O'Brien made 1938 a banner year for the Irish priest.

Tracy played Father Flanagan again in a sequel *Men of Boys Town* (1941), but, as is usually the case with sequels, it was less effective and popular than the original. In 1961, old and tired, Tracy played his last Irish priest, Father Matthew Doonan, in a piece of hokum about convicts, volcanic eruptions, and a rescue mission on a Pacific island entitled *The Devil at Four O'Clock.* The part is not very good, nor is Tracy at his best, but he brings flashes of authority to the role, and, like a time-worn monument, he is still impressive. In his last years as an actor, the Irish role for which Tracy is most likely to be remembered, however, is that of Mayor Frank Skeffington, the grand old political chieftain of John Ford's *The Last Hurrah* (1958).[35]

For all his initial reluctance to play a priest, Tracy later confessed to Garson Kanin that this role suited him best—priests "were always my most comfortable parts." Perhaps this attitude had something to do with his youthful feeling that he had a vocation for the priesthood. Katherine Hepburn, who knew Tracy very well for years, sensed that Tracy felt comfortable playing a priest. Although he was not a regular churchgoer and considered himself a "bad Catholic," Tracy remained deeply influenced by the religion in which he was raised.[36]

The concern with social issues that was characteristic of the Irish priest in the 1930s[37] was muted in the next decade but revived somewhat in the fifties and sixties. Karl Malden played tough priest Father Barry (based on the real-life character of Rev. John Corridan, S. J.) in *On the Waterfront* (1954), fighting crime and corruption on the New York-New Jersey docks, and Don Murray portrayed Father Charles Dismas Clark, S. J., in *The Hoodlum Priest* (1961), a Jesuit dedicated to rehabilitating criminal offenders in St. Louis. Although less hard boiled and involved than his fellow screen clerics, Tom Tryon's Father Stephen Fermoyle in *The Cardinal* (1963) was flogged by the Ku Klux Klan for his support of a black priest.

Another kind of Irish priest achieved widespread, if less durable, popularity in the 1940s, thanks to the cinematic genius of Leo McCarey (1898–1969). McCarey learned his craft with Hal Roach and made his mark as a director of screwball comedy in the thirties, winning an Oscar for *The Awful Truth* (1937). In *Going My Way* (1944), McCarey gave the audience a priest who was softer and more mellow than the tough priest, one more concerned with personal than public affairs, but one who was much more amusing and perhaps even more lovable—the humorous priest. Bing Crosby, the well-known crooner and star of musical and light comedy films, appeared as Father Chuck O'Malley, a charming troubleshooter ("Dial O for O'Malley") whom the Bishop sends to rescue the aged Father Fitzgibbon (Barry Fitzgerald, born William Shields) and his bankrupt parish, St. Dominic's. With the jocular encouragement of his clerical crony, Father O'Rourke (Frank McHugh), O'Malley sets to work resolving the problems of the parish and its people, and coming to terms with the crotchety but endearing old pastor. As an example of his magical touch, Father O'Malley converts a pack of juvenile delinquents into a marvelous parish glee club, whose nationwide tour provides the funds that save the day for St. Dominic's and Father Fitzgibbon. The film ends with Father O'Malley moving on to new challenges and Father O'Rourke assigned as Father Fitzgibbon's new curate. The happy ending continued at the box office when *Going My Way* proved to be the surprise hit of the year. It also won seven Academy Awards, including those for best picture, best actor (Crosby), and best supporting actor (Fitzgerald), as well as those for best story and direction (McCarey).

The laughter and human touches of McCarey's delightful soufflé provided ideal escapist fare for a nation at war, and its popular appeal is readily understandable. *Going My Way* did not treat contentious issues, such as religious doctrine or social questions. It hardly even touched on forms of worship; indeed, in essence the movie was neither Catholic nor especially religious. But it offered wit, humor, and marvelous character studies—particularly Fitzgerald's portrayal of Father Fitzgibbon: "senile, vain, childish, stubborn, good, bewildered, stupid—he is the quintessence of the pathos, dignity, and ludicrousness which old age can display."[38] In the midst of his wartime duties, John Ford took time to write Crosby a note of praise: "I hasten to write you about your truly great performance. Your scenes with Barry were the most beautiful I have ever seen on the screen. I sincerely admire you for your true spirit of teamwork and fair play. Perhaps that is why you emerge as a truly great artist."[39]

The enthusiastic reception given *Going My Way* brought about production of a sequel, *The Bells of St. Mary's* (1945), which continued the adventures of Crosby's Father O'Malley, replacing Fitzgerald with Ingrid Bergman as a wonderful nun. Among its notable scenes was one in which the children of St. Mary's parochial school recite the Pledge of Allegiance to the Flag, underlining the idea that Catholicism and Americanism are perfectly compatible. *The Bells of St. Mary's* did very well for a sequel, but Father O'Malley is more subdued and less playful than in *Going My Way,* and *St. Mary's* was not up to the mark set by its predecessor. There were no more Father O'Malley films, although *Going My Way* had a brief revival as a television series in 1962–1963, with Gene Kelly and Leo G. Carroll playing the parts made famous by Crosby and Fitzgerald. McCarey continued to produce, direct, and write films until 1962, but he never again achieved the success of *Going My Way.* Although teamed with Crosby in two more pictures, one of which was set in Ireland, Barry Fitzgerald (a Dublin-born Protestant) never again played a priest. The Irish-American

Catholic crooner did, although Crosby's attempt to create an older but still jaunty version of Father O'Malley in the pedestrian *Say One for Me* (1959) is not worth talking about.

Following his introduction as a major character by Tracy and O'Brien in the 1930s, the priest became a standard role in Hollywood movies, portrayed in a wide variety of nationalities by such talented actors as Gregory Peck, Henry Fonda, Montgomery Clift, Frank Sinatra, Jack Lemmon, Dana Andrews, Charles Boyer, William Holden, Clifton Webb, Robert Ryan, Robert De Niro, Richard Basehart, Thomas Mitchell, Edmund Gwenn, Cedric Hardwicke, Vincent Price, Charles Coburn, Preston Foster, Alan Hale, Ward Bond, Charles Bickford, Burgess Meredith, Van Johnson, Donald Crisp, Cecil Kellaway, Arthur Shields, John Huston, Basil van Ruysdael, Regis Toomey, William Demarest, Charles Durning,and Leif Erikson, among others. But it was the Irish priest who appeared most often on the screen—ministering to slum dwellers and social outcasts, to the casualties of war, and more recently to the well-off in our society. And the most familiar clerical character has remained the most popular, doing valuable service to those of his religion and ethnic origins, and to the nation in which he serves.

To their chagrin, Protestant ministers and Jewish rabbis did not receive equal treatment from the motion pictures. They complained to the PCA, but to no avail.[40] The studio bosses were not Catholic and had no particular fondness for Catholics or their clergy. But they did know (once it was demonstrated to them) what made good box office. And they were doubtless aware that the Legion of Decency would never complain about too many priests in pictures, provided they were always depicted favorably.[41]

The Irish priest, although endowed with highly individual characteristics by the performer who portrayed him, was a stereotype. As with other stereotypes, this meant that his character had some basis in reality but that the reality was distorted for dramatic effect. A number of other stereotypes besides priests and antiheroes made up Hollywood's gallery of Irish characters in the 1930s. As these were well established before movies came along, the new medium simply took them over. There was the saintly long-suffering mother (almost every Irish movie family had one); the beautiful, fiery colleen; the dashing adventurer; the romantic troubadour (more popular in the forties); the policeman or military noncommissioned officer; and the comic boyos and biddies—buzzing, boozing, blustering, or bumbling, and sometimes doing all of these at once.

The Irish also frequently played or were depicted as prizefighters, journalists, and politicians, but they had no monopoly on these roles. In fact, most of the Irish character types mentioned were roles common to other ethnic groups, including WASPs. This was not true of the priest, of course; nor was it true of cops, army sergeants, or boyos who blarney and booze. The boyo is definitely an Irish stereotype designed to provide comic relief, although this was sometimes overdone, especially in John Ford's films. By the 1930s the Irish had been the backbone of the police force in most major Northern cities for decades, and the Irish cop was a familiar figure in real life as in reel life. Firemen were probably even more heavily Irish, but their screen appearances were infrequent because they were harder to make use of. The Irish also provided a large number of men for the armed services, and since the officer corps was still small and mostly WASP, the Irish usually rose no higher than top sergeant.

If one examines a representative group of Irish actors and actresses in this period, one finds that there are more of the former than the latter because movies, then as now, offered more parts for men. One also finds that supporting players were more often cast in Irish parts than were leading men or ladies. Of the well-known Irish leading men of the thirties, Australian-born Errol Flynn was typecast as a swashbuckling adventurer, but with the exception of his roles in *Captain Blood* (1935), *Dodge City* (1939), and *Gentleman Jim* (1942), the life of former heavyweight boxing champion James J. Corbett, the adventurers Flynn played were usually English or American. If one adds occasional Latin roles, the same was true of Tyrone Power, the last of a long line of Irish actors bearing that name, whose only Irish role in the 1930s was that of Dion O'Leary in *In Old Chicago* (1937). Tenors John MacCormack and Morton Downey played troubadours in early sound films, but their talent did not extend to acting, and their motion picture careers were mercifully brief. Former vaudevillian George Murphy was more successful, playing a cheerful song-and-dance man in a series of musicals before shifting to dramatic parts after World War II. Ronald Reagan, more a second lead than a star in his early Hollywood years (1937–1942), almost always played an All-American boy, notably in the small but pivotal role of George Gipp, "The Gipper," in *Knute Rockne, All American*. Irish-born George Brent (George Brendan Nolan) was best known for playing self-effacing male leads in Bette Davis pictures, but he did a creditable job as "Wild Bill" Donovan, the heroic commander of *The Fighting 69th*. For Irish male stars in Irish roles, audiences would have to depend largely on James Cagney, Pat O'Brien, and, occasionally, Spencer Tracy.

Although Maureen O'Hara (FitzSimons) became the quintessential colleen because of her Irish origins and breathtaking beauty, it took the heroine of John Ford's *The Quiet Man* (1952) thirteen years in American movies before she achieved that identification. Her most important early role was that of Angharad Morgan in Ford's story of a Welsh mining family, *How Green Was My Valley* (1941). In the decade that followed, O'Hara played a variety of heroines in historical epics and contemporary dramas, a number of which were filmed in Technicolor to highlight her red hair and peaches-and-cream complexion.

An Irish star who did play Irish roles in the thirties and forties was Barbara Stanwyck.[42] Stanwyck played Nora Clitheroe in John Ford's screen version of Sean O'Casey's *The Plough and the Stars* (1937), and she also played the feisty heroine Mollie Monahan in Cecil B. DeMille's Western epic *Union Pacific* (1939). In 1942 Stanwyck won an Oscar nomination for her performance as the riotous stripper Sugarpuss O'Shea in Howard Hawk's screwball comedy *Ball of Fire* (1941). Although she didn't win the Academy Award (nominated four times, she never won), Stanwyck proved that Irish girls, while often high-spirited were not necessarily virginal. In 1987 she was honored with the American Film Institute's Life Achievement Award for her outstanding work on the screen.

Ann Sheridan, who played opposite James Cagney three times, was another example of a "good bad" Irish girl. Of mixed Irish, Scottish, and Cherokee ancestry, this Texas colleen became the female counterpart of Cagney's antihero: cynical and tough on the surface, vulnerable underneath. Her best role was that of hoydenish Randy Monaghan in *King's Row* (1942), whose warmth and strength sustain her lover Drake McHugh (Ronald Reagan, also in his best part) after he has lost both legs as the result of an

accident. For Irish femmes fatales, who were all bad and unre-
deemable, there were the treacherous Brigid O'Shaughnessy (Mary
Astor) in *The Maltese Falcon* (1941) and the equally insidious Kitty
Collins (Ava Gardner) in *The Killers* (1946). Even with colleens,
beauty might conceal a black heart.

Easily the most versatile Irish leading lady of the 1930s and
1940s was the lovely Irene Dunne, who played successfully in musicals—*Roberta* (1935), *Show Boat* (1936); screwball comedies—
Theodora Goes Wild (1936), *The Awful Truth* (1937); and heavy
dramas—*Cimarron* (1931), *Love Affair* (1939). In 1948 she gave
a marvelous performance in the title role of *I Remember Mama*;
but alas, Mama was Norwegian American and Irene Dunne never
played an Irish role in her twenty-two years of making movies,
nor did she ever win the coveted Oscar, despite her five nomina-
tions.

Rosalind Russell also failed in her four tries at the award, but
she, too, was a notable success as an actress. Although she did
well in dramatic roles, Russell's real forte was comedy, and her
most memorable roles were Sylvia in *The Women* (1939), Hildy
Johnson in *His Girl Friday* (1940), Ruth McKenny in *My Sister
Eileen* (1942), and Mame in *Auntie Mame* (1958). Russell's sense
of humor and *joie de vivre* were as evident in her personal life as
in her work as a comedienne. Both she and Irene Dunne were
prominent members of Hollywood's Catholic community.

Although she has been much more active on the stage than the
screen, Helen Hayes (Helen Hayes Brown) proved very effective
in the films in which she did appear, winning an Oscar for a straight
dramatic role in *The Sin of Madelon Claudet* (1931) and for a
semicomic performance in *Airport* (1970). Her only real Irish role,
however, was in *My Son John* (1953), Leo McCarey's anti-Communist polemic.

Entering films in 1930, lovely Irish-born Maureen O'Sullivan
played a variety of non-Irish roles, becoming best known as Tar-
zan's mate Jane in MGM's popular series of jungle films. After
marrying director John Farrow, she retired from the screen in 1942
to raise a large family (which included daughter Mia Farrow) and
returned to the screen only occasionally thereafter.

Among supporting actresses, Sara Allgood, of Dublin's Abbey
Players, achieved her greatest fame in mother roles, most memor-

ably as Mrs. Morgan in John Ford's *How Green Was My Valley* (1941). Aline MacMahon tackled a wide range of roles in her long career, from a fortune-hunting chorine in *Gold Diggers of 1933* (1933) to a wise grandaunt in *All the Way Home* (1963). Her remarkable staying power is evidence of considerable talent. Although she made relatively few pictures, Barbara O'Neil also played a variety of parts, but she is best remembered for her fine performance as Ellen O'Hara, Scarlett's beloved and unselfish mother, in *Gone with the Wind*. Rita Johnson (McSean) specialized in "other woman" parts, such as Ginger Rogers' rival in *The Major and the Minor* (1942) and Charles Laughton's doomed mistress in *The Big Clock* (1948). Gail Patrick (Margaret Fitzpatrick) also often played the "other woman," for example, Carole Lombard's nasty sister in *My Man Godfrey* (1936). Ruth Hussey (O'Rourke) portrayed sophisticated and witty ladies, parts similar to those played by Rosalind Russell, except that Hussey was usually cast as a second lead. Her most memorable role was probably that of the magazine photographer in *The Philadelphia Story* (1940). If Mary Boland did not invent the flighty, featherbrained society matron, she certainly perfected the character in movies like *Ruggles of Red Gap* (1935) and *The Women* (1939). Florenz Ziegfeld's widow Billie Burke brought her own delightful brand of scatterbrained comedy to the screen, but she gained immortality as Glinda, the Good Witch of the North, in *The Wizard of Oz* (1939). Irene Ryan (Riordan), who later won fame as Granny in television's "Beverly Hillbillies," usually appeared in comic duo with her husband Tim Ryan. Una O'Connor (Agnes Teresa McGlade), another Abbey player, turned in a strong performance as the sorrowing mother in John Ford's *The Informer*, but she is better remembered for playing the archetypal biddy in a succession of films in the 1930s and 1940s.

Most familiar to audiences in the category of Irish supporting actresses were the wise-cracking "tough cookies," who were never without a comment or a comeback during the Depression decade and the war that followed. Among the most prominent of these lively ladies were Glenda Farrell, Patsy Kelly, Helen Broderick (Broderick Crawford's mother), Ruth Donnelly, Dorothy McNulty (later Penny Singleton of "Blondie" fame), and Martha Raye (Margaret O'Reed). They brightened the screen and the lives of the audience in many a movie, often helping to rescue second-rate films from the panning they deserved.

The roster of supporting actors in the thirties is a long one and includes many identified with Irish roles. A few highly versatile character actors played many different parts: Walter Brennan, J. Carrol Naish, Thomas Mitchell, Brian Donlevy, and Walter Connolly. Born in Massachusetts of Irish parents, Brennan was the first performer to win three Oscars, but in a film career that lasted more than forty years, he never played an Irish role. Naish, a master of foreign accents, played almost every nationality but Irish, being deemed unsuitable for Irish parts because of his dark complexion.[43] On the one occasion when he did play an Irishman, General Phil Sheridan in John Ford's *Rio Grande* (1950), Naish's stolid performance offers no hint that the character is Irish. Gruff Walter Connolly appeared in many roles, including that of the famous Irish composer in *The Great Victor Herbert* (1939), but he is probably best remembered as Claudette Colbert's millionaire father in Frank Capra's delightful comedy *It Happened One Night* (1934). Although not restricted to Irish parts, Thomas Mitchell was often cast in them. His most memorable Irish roles, along with the one that made Brian Donlevy a star, are described later.

Among the more "Irish" character actors, there was a certain amount of specialization. In the cops, noncoms, and other "tough guys" category, often played with comic overtones, could be found: boisterous Alan Hale (McKahan); glib, fast-talking Lee Tracy; the wonderfully irascible James Gleason; deadpan Tom Dugan; cheery Dick Foran and James Dunn; quiet, reliable William Gargan, Regis Toomey, James Burke, and Robert Emmet O'Connor; dumbbells Ed Brophy, Ed Gargan, Tom Kennedy, Horace MacMahon, and Allen Jenkins (McConegal); hard-boiled, sarcastic Barton MacLane, Paul Kelly, Jerome Cowan, Pat Flaherty, James Flavin, and Harry Shannon; and those unforgettable masters of the double-take and the "slow burn," Edgar Kennedy and Donald MacBride. Starting in the "tough guys" category were some actors talented and lucky enough to move up to leading roles, among them Lloyd Nolan, Edmond O'Brien, Broderick Crawford (Pendergast), and Dennis O'Keefe (Edward Flanagan). As perennial boyos there were boozy James Barton, rascally J. M. Kerrigan, blustering Victor McLaglen, convivial Frank McHugh, gravel-voiced

Tim Ryan, sourpuss William Frawley, and, of course, Barry Fitzgerald, the archetypal boyo before his appearance in *Going My Way*. Fitzgerald's equally talented younger brother, Arthur Shields, demonstrated an easy mastery over a wide range of more subdued roles. For comic relief, pure and simple, there were timid, fussy Victor Moore and Jimmy Conlin, gregarious Lloyd Corrigan, dizzy Jack Haley (the Tinman in *The Wizard of Oz*), bibulous Jack Norton, the movies' most famous drunk (who never imbibed offscreen), and nervous, bumbling Eddie Foy, Jr., who sometimes played his famous father, as in *Yankee Doodle Dandy*.

Behind the camera was another of Eddie Foy's sons, producer-director Bryan "Brynie" Foy, who made a name for himself as "Keeper of the B's," the quickie films turned out by studios that filled the bottom half of a double feature. James Kevin McGuinness did several screenplays for John Ford and then began producing films for MGM. William McGann, James P. Hogan, and Ralph Murphy directed B's, whereas Elliot Nugent specialized in romantic comedies. Raoul Walsh, who started in films as an assistant director to D. W. Griffith and played John Wilkes Booth in *The Birth of a Nation,* was in the front rank of directors by the thirties. His specialty was action-packed films starring actors such as Errol Flynn and James Cagney.

In the writing department there was W(illiam) R(iley) Burnett, a successful novelist of Irish-Welsh descent, whose book *Little Caesar* (1930) launched the gangster film cycle of the Depression era. Over the next three decades a number of Burnett's other works were adapted for the screen. He himself helped adapt some of them, including *High Sierra* (1941) and *Captain Lightfoot* (1955), as well as coauthoring scripts for a variety of other movies, notably *Scarface* (1932), *Wake Island* (1942), and *The Great Escape* (1963). Philip Dunne, the son of "Mr. Dooley's" creator, Finley Peter Dunne, also made a name for himself as a scenarist in the talkies; he is best known for his work on *How Green Was My Valley*. John Meehan went from Broadway to Hollywood to write a number of successful screenplays, including that of *Boys Town*. John Patrick (Goggan) got his start as a scenarist for B movies. In the forties he graduated to "A" features and then became a successful playwright (*The Hasty Heart, Teahouse of the August Moon*) whose works were later filmed. Walter Plunkett began a long career as a costume designer in 1933, as did the famous "Irene" (Irene Gibbons) in 1938. Irish songwriters also did well in Hollywood. Composer Jimmy McHugh wrote hits such as "Don't Blame Me" and "I'm in the Mood for Love," and lyricist Johnny Burke won an Oscar for "Swinging on a Star" from *Going My Way.* Composer Robert Emmett Dolan, who moved from Broadway to Hollywood in 1941, proved highly successful as a music director, scoring such popular films as *Holiday Inn* (1942) and *The Bells of St. Mary's.* Although he never won an Oscar, Dolan was nominated for one eight times during the forties.

There were a considerable number of "Irish movies" in the 1930s. Most of them were produced by Warner Bros., the "New Deal studio," where contemporary urban life and social problems were the subject for many films. Cagney and O'Brien movies were usually "Irish," whatever the title, and the studio often used titles that made the subject explicit: *The Irish in Us* (1935), *The Great O'Malley* (1937), *Three Cheers for the Irish* (1940), and *The Fighting 69th* (1940). In the first of these, Cagney, O'Brien, and Frank McHugh played the three O'Hara brothers: a prizefight manager, a policeman, and a fireman, respectively. Whereas Cagney and O'Brien are after the same girl, the comedy centers on the brothers' interaction and their relationship with their darlin' Irish mother (Mary Gordon). *The Great O'Malley* has O'Brien as an overzealous cop who helps send an innocent man to jail but redeems his error by securing the victim's release.

Three Cheers for the Irish features Thomas Mitchell as Officer Peter Casey, the father of three daughters who must contend not only with unwanted retirement from the N.Y.C. police force but with the daunting prospect of a Scottish son-in-law, Angus Ferguson, a rookie cop whose burr is as thick as Casey's brogue. Casey resolves his retirement problem by going into politics and being elected an alderman after an uproarious campaign. He is reconciled to daughter Maureen's marriage to Angus when she gives birth to twins, although he does rush off at the film's end seeking Father Monahan "to make this thing legal," after he learns that Maureen and Angus were wed by a justice of the peace. The movie is replete with such broad touches of Irish humor, as well as lovable stereotypes, and the result is a first-rate comedy. Thomas Mitchell does his usual outstanding job as Officer-Candidate-Alderman Casey, and he gets a needed reminder about tolerance from American-born Maureen when he protests her dating Angus:

Casey: How many times have you been out with this—this immigrant?

Maureen (defiantly): A lot! (with spirit)—and he's no more of an immigrant than you are.

Casey (shocked): What is it you're talkin' about? Ain't he a Scotchman just fresh off the boat?

Maureen: He's been here since nineteen-thirty—and you came off the boat the same as he did, and he's as much of an American citizen as you are.

Casey (stunned): I never thought I'd live to hear my daughter comparin' me unfavorably with a Scotchman.

Maureen: Pop, it's about time you got it straight that there isn't any room in this country for inter-racial feuds. Unless he's an Indian, everyone in this country is either an immigrant or descended from one.

Casey (roaring): Oh . . . You've been listenin' to them radicals, eh?

Maureen: I haven't been listening to anyone—except you. And you've always been hounding me to get a boy friend. Well, I've got one—and look what happens.

This exchange evokes memories of the Irish-Jewish intermarriage films, and *Three Cheers for the Irish* might be appropriately subtitled "Angus's Irish Rose."

The Fighting 69th trotted out Warners' whole stable of Irish actors to tell the story of New York's famous Irish regiment in World War I. In addition to Cagney, O'Brien, and George Brent, there were Alan Hale, Frank McHugh, Dick Foran, William Lundigan, Henry O'Neill, Tom Dugan, James Flavin, and Frank Faylen. The Irish-Jewish connection, so popular in the 1920s, was represented by Sammy Cohen, who identifies himself as "Mike Murphy" to enlist in the 69th. When "Mike" lies dying in France, Father Duffy (O'Brien) recites the Jewish prayer for the dying in Hebrew to comfort him.[44]

At Warners, virtually everybody got into the Irish act. Dennis Morgan (Stanley Morner), a Norwegian American, looked Irish, sounded Irish, and sometimes played Irish parts, for example, Chauncey Olcott in *My Wild Irish Rose* (1947). Even Humphrey

Bogart joined in, playing Bette Davis's moody, insolent stablemaster, Michael O'Leary, in *Dark Victory* (1939). The part does not do Bogart justice and vice versa; the casting is especially ironic when one considers that the other male principals in the film, George Brent and Ronald Reagan, were both playing WASP characters.

Other studios paid less attention to the Irish. In addition to *San Francisco* and the two *Boys Town* movies, MGM did *The Bowery* (1933), with Wallace Beery and George Raft as two arch-rival Irish saloonkeepers, and adapted George M. Cohan's musical play *Little Nellie Kelly* (1940) for Judy Garland and George Murphy. The studio's most ambitious Irish project, *Parnell* (1937), was also its biggest flop. The "King of Hollywood," Clark Gable portrayed Charles Stewart Parnell, the "Uncrowned King of Ireland." Parnell's leadership of the Irish nationalist movement in the 1880s, his ill-starred love affair with Kitty O'Shea, and his tragic fall from power and death had been made into a compelling stage drama that did well in London and New York. But in making the transition to the screen, *Parnell* lost its appeal, partly because of its star. Gable wanted to play the part, but he knew almost nothing about Parnell and was not at all like him; he even played the role without a beard. From beginning to end, Gable lacked conviction as Parnell, and the film was one of the few box office failures of his long career. MGM also made the successful *Dr. Kildare* and *Maisie* series, with Lew Ayres and Ann Sothern playing Jim Kildare and "Maisie" (Mary Anastasia O'Connor), but little was made of the Irish ancestry of either character.

Although Tyrone Power became 20th Century-Fox's leading male star in the late 1930s, production chief Darryl F. Zanuck made almost no use of him in Irish roles, despite Power's heritage and "black Irish" good looks. The one exception was Zanuck's answer to MGM's *San Francisco: In Old Chicago* (1937), a fictional portrayal of the O'Leary family, whose cow supposedly started the great fire of 1871. Alice Brady won an Oscar for her role as the hard-working widowed mother, Mrs. O'Leary, and Power, Don Ameche, and Tom Brown were her three sons. Although Ameche was not a priest, he played the moralist to Power's engaging "black sheep," Dion O'Leary. In the conflagration that forms the picture's climax, Ameche is killed and Power redeemed, to play what one is certain will be a leading part in the rebuilding of Chicago, as Gable assuredly would do in San Francisco after his salvation. The movie could have been subtitled "Life with the O'Learys," and there is enough blarney, sentiment, high jinks, and melodramatic action to satisfy even the AOH.

Paramount's principal Irish contribution was made at the end of the decade with *Union Pacific* (1939) and *The Great McGinty* (1940). The latter was scenarist Preston Sturges' first attempt at direction. The story, written by Sturges, told of the meteoric rise and fall of one Dan McGinty, an Irish vagabond who joins a corrupt political machine to become first mayor, then governor, but who turns honest and has to flee to a "banana republic" with his cohorts. Brian Donlevy was excellent as McGinty, as was Akim Tamiroff as a decidedly non-Irish political boss. A low-budget film, *The Great McGinty* turned out to be a "sleeper," doing very well at the box office and winning Sturges an Oscar for original screenplay. It also made Donlevy a star and helped in his conversion from villian to "good guy;" almost always a "bad guy" before *McGinty*, he rarely played one afterward. It seems appropriate that the Irish-born actor's big break came through his portrayal of a crooked but lovable Irish politician. Cecil B. DeMille's *Union Pacific*, which featured Donlevy as principal (and non-Irish villain), was a rousing epic about the building of the first transcontinental railroad in the years just following the Civil War. The movie is big on budget, action, and thrills, and its cast abounds with Irish characters, from heroine Molly Monahan (Barbara Stanwyck) to engineers, foremen, and tracklayers. Although the Irish are depicted as sometimes irresponsible, being too fond of whiskey and gambling and needing a firm WASP hand to keep them at work, DeMille and screenwriter C. Gardner Sullivan do pay tribute to the vital contribution made by Irish spirit and brawn to our national expansion.[45]

In addition to John Ford's Irish films, *The Informer* (1935) and *The Plough and the Stars* (1936),[46] RKO offered *Kitty Foyle* (1940), the screen adaptation of Christopher Morley's popular novel about the romantic trials and tribulations of the working girl. The film is basically a soap opera, but it does show something of the problems that arise when a poor Irish girl falls in love with a rich WASP from Philadelphia's Main Line. Ginger Rogers gave a sensitive performance as the resilient heroine, which won her an Academy Award.

Universal Pictures, which specialized in horror movies and Deanna Durbin musicals in the 1930s, dramatized the life of one of the most colorful characters of the Gilded Age in *Diamond Jim* (1935). Edward Arnold gave a winning performance as James Buchanan Brady, the gourmandizing financier who carried on a love affair with the toast of Broadway, Lillian Russell. Arnold was equally impressive when he repeated the role in *Lillian Russell* (1940).

Beloved Enemy (1936), an independent production by Samuel Goldwyn, is one of the most intriguing—and exasperating—movies ever made about Ireland. This account of the Anglo-Irish struggle of 1919–1921 and its tragic aftermath is an amazing blend of fact and fiction. Its hero is Dennis Riordan (Brian Aherne), a rebel leader closely modeled on the legendary Michael Collins, and a number of incidents in the film are based on historical fact. But when the narrative diverges from the historical record, it goes to extremes, as with Riordan's falling in love with the daughter of an influential British peer. At the end of the movie, Riordan, like Collins, is shot by nationalist diehards who oppose the peace treaty he has signed with the British. Collins died, a tragic loss for Ireland, and so did Riordan—at least he did when the movie opened in New York City. But Goldwyn had hedged his bets by filming two endings, and when the audience responded unfavorably to the hero's death, the second ending replaced the first, and it remains the one shown to this day. In the revised version, just when Riordan seems about to expire, he turns to his aristocratic English sweetheart to declare: "It's all right, darlin'; I'm not going to die. A good Irishman never does what's expected of him." This concession to the public preference for happy endings, although understandable, mars one of the very few motion pictures to deal with a critical and complex period in Irish history. The ludicrous parts of *Beloved Enemy* contrast sharply with those that are dramatically valid and historically sound; and one laments the film's shortcomings because of its virtues.[47]

In reviewing the films of the thirties (and forties), one should not overlook the families that appeared in individual motion pictures or in series: the Monaghans of *King's Row* (Ann Sheridan,

Ernest Cossart, and Pat Moriarity), the O'Riordans of *My Son, My Son* (1940) (Laraine Day, Henry Hull, and others), the Higginses (1938–1941) (James, Lucille, and Russell Gleason), and the McGuerins of Brooklyn (1942–1943) (William Bendix and Grace Bradley).[48]

The most famous Irish screen family of the 1930s appeared in the greatest movie of the decade and perhaps of all time—the O'Haras of *Gone with the Wind* (1939). *GWTW* was David O. Selznick's spectacular adaptation of Margaret Mitchell's runaway best-seller about the destruction of the Old South during the Civil War and Reconstruction Era. While it is true that the Irish were much more numerous in the North than in the South, there were tens of thousands who lived in Dixie; 40 thousand Irish immigrants fought for the Confederacy,[49] and Margaret Mitchell was herself of Irish descent. The movie's antihero, Rhett Butler (Clark Gable), bears a name long associated with Ireland, for the Butlers were one of the great Norman clans of that country. More important, the antiheroine is Scarlett O'Hara (Vivien Leigh), the daughter of a genteel French creole from Louisiana and an exuberant Irish Catholic immigrant, Gerald O'Hara, whose Georgia plantation "Tara" is named after the famous Hill of Kings in Ireland. It is her father who passes on to "Katie Scarlett" his own love of Tara, an Irish peasant's fierce and abiding love for the land: "Why land is the only thing worth working for, worth fighting for, worth dying for, because it's the only thing that lasts." To Gerald O'Hara, it is unthinkable that anyone with a drop of Irish blood could feel otherwise. And in Scarlett's case, time proves him right. Thomas Mitchell played this role to the hilt, and Barbara O'Neil was a tower of love and strength as Scarlett's mother, Ellen. Scarlett O'Hara and Rhett Butler are fascinating characters and much too complex to be labeled stereotypes; yet they bear more than a passing resemblance to those of the fiery, beautiful colleen and the dashing adventurer. For outright villainy in the film there is Johnny Gallagher (J. M. Kerrigan), the supplier and overseer of convict labor in Scarlett's lumber mill and a black-hearted rogue. From beginning to end, the Irish loom large in *Gone with the Wind*.

As the Irish forged ahead in Hollywood, so they moved ahead in society as supporters and beneficiaries of the New Deal. Irish politicians and voters were an integral part of the nation's ruling

Democratic coalition. FDR appointed Irish Catholics to his Cabinet and the Supreme Court, and he named Joe Kennedy ambassador to the Court of St. James's. Irish Catholics were also prominent leaders of the AFL and the CIO in the newly powerful labor movement. The Catholic church, under Irish control, was now almost a part of the American establishment. Spencer Tracy and James Cagney were already big stars, and John Ford was on his way to becoming the greatest American director since D. W. Griffith.

1. *Peg o' My Heart* (Laurette Taylor) (1922)

2. *Irene* (Kate Price, Colleen Moore, and Charlie Murray) (1926)

3. *The Cohens and the Kellys* (Charlie Murray and Kate Price on the right) (1926)

4. *The Public Enemy* (Mae Clarke and James Cagney) (1931)

5. *Angels with Dirty Faces* (James Cagney and Pat O'Brien) (1938)

6. *San Francisco* (Clark Gable, Jack Holt, Spencer Tracy, and Jeannette MacDonald) (1936)

7. *Boys Town* (Spencer Tracy) (1938)

8. *Going My Way* (Bing Crosby and Barry Fitzgerald) (1944)

9. *Parnell* (Clark Gable and Myrna Loy) (1937)

10. *In Old Chicago* (Tyrone Power and Alice Brady) (1937)

11. *The Informer* (Victor McLaglen and Wallace Ford) (1935)

12. *The Quiet Man* (Maureen O'Hara, Victor McLaglen, John Wayne, and Barry Fitzgerald) (1952)

13. *The Last Hurrah* (Edward Brophy, Spencer Tracy, Pat O'Brien, James Gleason, and Ricardo Cortez) (1958)

14. *The Fighting 69th* (Pat O'Brien, George Brent, James Cagney, and Alan Hale) (1940)

15. *Yankee Doodle Dandy* (Jeanne Cagney, James Cagney, Joan Leslie, Walter Huston, and Rosemary DeCamp) (1942)

16. *A Tree Grows in Brooklyn* (Peggy Ann Garner, James Dunn, Ted Donaldson, and Dorothy McGuire) (1944)

17. *A Tree Grows in Brooklyn* (James Dunn and James Gleason) (1944)

18. *My Son John* (Robert Walker, Dean Jagger, and Helen Hayes) (1952)

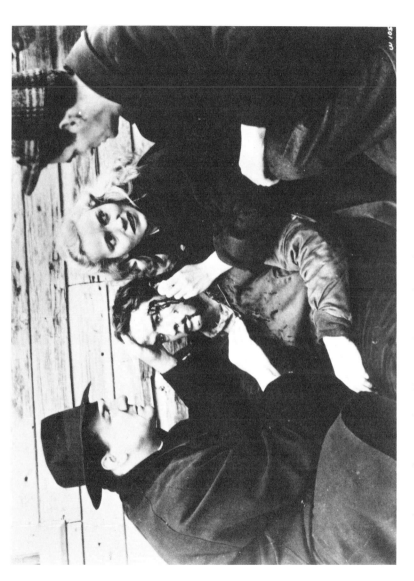

19. *On the Waterfront* (Karl Malden, Marlon Brando, and Eva Marie Saint) (1954)

20. *High Society* (Grace Kelly) (1956)

21. *An American in Paris* (Gene Kelly) (1951)

22. *The Molly Maguires* (Richard Harris and Sean Connery) (1970)

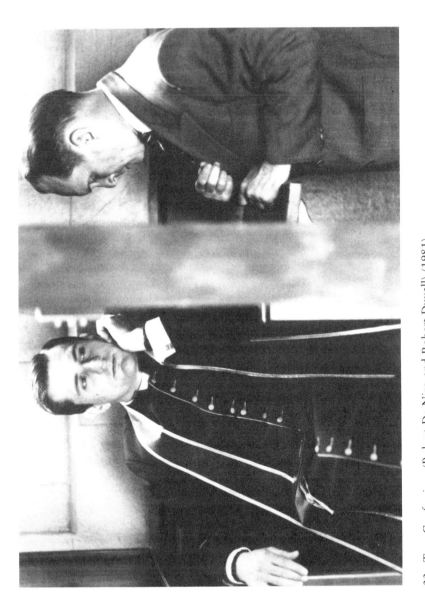

23. *True Confessions* (Robert De Niro and Robert Duvall) (1981)

24. *Ragtime* (James Cagney) (1981)

John Ford: Irish Nonpareil

More than fifteen years after his death, John Ford (1894–1973) remains pre-eminent among American motion picture directors of the sound era, the only one to win six Academy Awards and four New York Film Critics Awards for his work, and the first recipient of the American Film Institute's prestigious Life Achievement Award. Although he is best known for his Westerns, Ford's Irish films also form an important part of his oeuvre. They merit examination for what they reveal about Ford's ethnic heritage and the ways it influenced his portrayal of Irish and non-Irish characters. In these movies Ford tells us a great deal about himself and the values that sustained the Irish on both sides of the Atlantic.

Any discussion of the man and his work should be prefaced, however, by a frank admission that John Ford is far from being an easy subject. A great deal of what he said about his life and work is contradicted by documented facts, by himself, or by both. Whether on account of a desire to amuse, confound, outrage, or gratify his own ego, or simply because of inaccurate perception or failure to recall, Ford's version of things is quite often unreliable. His cavalier disregard for accuracy and consistency is but one aspect of a personality composed of such sharply contrasting traits as to make Ford seem an almost Jekyll-and-Hyde character. John Ford was a sensitive man, one capable of acts of great kindness, but he was often cruel and malicious, not only to hapless interviewers, but also to family, friends, and close associates. He was a man of deep religious convictions, whose personal life was far from exemplary. Although very intelligent and well read, Ford liked to portray himself as a cultural illiterate. He dismissed movies as nothing more than a well-paid job, ridiculed the notion that he was an "artist," and professed indifference to the awards bestowed on him. Yet he loved making movies, cared deeply about what others thought of his work, and displayed his Oscars proudly. Plagued by alcoholism, Ford maintained a rigid self-discipline that kept work and drink separate until late in his career. To some extent, and perhaps to a large extent, Ford's split personality was the product of his ethnic heritage and youthful experience.[1]

John Ford grew up in Portland, Maine, the tenth of eleven children of John and Barbara (Curran) Feeney, both immigrants from County Galway.[2] From his parents, especially his mother, he inherited the austere Catholicism that played such a vital part in Irish life and was to affect his own work profoundly. As a saloonkeeper, Ford's father was a central figure in Portland's Irish community, for social drinking was an important rite for the Irish in America as it was for those in Ireland. In that community, young John learned the songs, stories, customs, and militant nationalism that made up his Hibernian heritage. He also learned to speak Gaelic and remained fluent in that tongue throughout his life.[3] Beginning in his childhood, Ford made a number of visits to Ireland, and his experience there served to reinforce his sense of ethnic identity. At the same time, his heritage and background exposed him to the prejudice of Portland's WASP community. This kind of experience aroused his resentment, but it also left him with feelings of personal insecurity and strengthened his desire to prove himself a good American.[4]

From Ford's early life stemmed his preoccupation with the themes that characterized his movies, those about America as well as Ireland.[5] Prominent among them was the central importance of the community—family, ship, regiment, village, town, and so on: its traditions and relationship with outsiders. Ford's Irish and Catholic background gave him a reverence for community and tradition, but this conservatism was countered by a rebel streak that was also part of his Irish and immigrant heritage. In his films, the individual was not helpless, not predestined, but he could achieve salvation only through the community. To further the common cause, he might dissent, but only within carefully defined limits, lest he put himself beyond the pale. The tension between conservatism and rebellion is evident in Ford's American films, in which he criticizes as well as celebrates the mythology of the Old West. Such criticism is largely lacking in his Irish pictures, however, probably because sentimentality and nostalgia colored his view of life on the "Ould Sod."

Whatever Ford's approach to his subject, it was generally lightened by humor, which he considered his forte.[6] Ford felt that in every dramatic or tragic scene, there was always a chance to slip in a little comedy. "The two play against each other. Tragedy is very close to comedy."[7] Humor relieved narrative tension and sometimes saved his films from becoming ponderous and overly sentimental.[8] For comedy in his Irish and some of his other films, Ford relied on the well-defined "stage Irishman" in his various guises. In fact, Ford may have done more than anyone else in Hollywood to perpetuate Irish stereotypes, particularly that of the hard-drinking boyo. His insistence on the importance of drinking as a ritual of male companionship was primarily the product of his ethnic and family heritage. Social and often excessive drinking figures prominently in almost all his films. Although often successful in employing this kind of broad humor, Ford sometimes overdid the boozing, bantering, and brawling, leading even sympathetic critics to complain.[9]

Most of Ford's pictures during the silent era were Westerns, and he made only a handful of films about the Irish. All were mediocre, and all were made for Fox (where Ford worked closely with Winnie Sheehan) except for *The Prince of Avenue A* (Universal, 1920). The only thing noteworthy about this film was its star, "Gentleman Jim" Corbett, the former heavyweight boxing champion. At fifty-four, the man who took the ring crown from the legendary John L. Sullivan in 1892 was a trifle old to play the romantic hero, Barry O'Connor, but the movie did provide Corbett the opportunity to display his pugilistic skills as he vanquished his ungentlemanly opponents at a society ball. There is not much Irish about *Shamrock Handicap* (1926), except for its beginning and ending in County Kildare and the comic relief provided by J. Farrell MacDonald as Con O'Shea, a faithful family retainer. Most of the story takes place in America, including the exciting steeplechase that forms the climax. Brilliantly shot and edited, this sequence almost makes up for the lack of action in the rest of the movie. MacDonald appears again in *Riley the Cop* (1928), and his endearing portrayal of Riley is the only good thing about the film.[10] To some degree a stereotype, with his big feet, thirst for alcoholic beverages, and penchant for Irish phrases, Riley also has humor, compassion, and common sense, all of which help to carry him successfully through a series of comic escapades in America and Europe. *Mother Machree* (1928) is a routine tearjerker about mother love and sacrifice. *Hangman's House* (1928), a melodrama laid in Ireland during the rebellion of 1919–1921, is notable for its somber, doom-laden aura. In its time frame, mood, and use of Victor McLaglen as its protagonist, *Hangman's House* foreshadows *The Informer*, but there the similarity ends. The story is sentimental, the acting mediocre, and the direction uninspired, except for a steeplechase that recalls the one in *Shamrock Handicap*, anticipates the one in *The Quiet Man*, and features a newcomer who would star in the latter film and many other Ford pictures—John Wayne.[11]

The Informer (1935) was Ford's first sound film about Ireland, produced at RKO on a shoestring with only the grudging assent of the studio bosses. Ford wanted to make this film very much, enjoyed making it, and greatly enhanced his reputation as a result. In retrospect, however, he claimed that it was not one of his favorite pictures because it lacked humor.[12] The story of a man who betrays his best friend is not one that lends itself to comedy, and Ford was wise to minimize it. Aside from this constraint and that of a budget of $243,000, Ford was free to shape the film to his taste. And he did so, reworking both Liam O'Flaherty's novel and Dudley Nichols' script until they satisfied him,[13] and manipulating Victor McLaglen into a fine performance as the tormented and desperate informer, Gypo Nolan.

Working under primitive conditions, Ford made a virtue of necessity, using low-key lighting and fog to mask fake backdrops and accentuate the story's nightmarish character. The film's pervasive darkness and shadows portend the doom of the informer, as the fog that surrounds him symbolizes his confusion. Having been expelled from the Irish Republican Army for insubordination, Gypo is hunted down and killed by his former comrades when he becomes an informer, an offense that makes even his British paymasters scorn him. The leitmotif of guilt, repentance, and absolution (by the mother of Gypo's victim) shows the strong influence of Ford's Catholicism, whereas the director's militant nationalism is reflected in the romanticized picture of the IRA and in the film's haunting street ballads and (somewhat intrusive) musical score. The love of Gypo's victim for his mother and sister and their grief at his death do honor to the family, and respectful treatment is accorded community rituals, such as the victim's wake and the IRA's trial of the informer. From beginning to end, the film stresses the overriding importance of the community—the nation, the IRA—and the inevitable destruction of those who violate its code.

In contrast to most of Ford's later movies, the style of *The Informer* is expressionistic rather than realistic, and its symbolism seems heavy-handed today. But it should be remembered that the film's budget precluded social realism, that expressionism was well suited to the story, and that Ford's approach was highly praised at the time and for some years thereafter. It should also be recalled that Ford was not trying to recreate the harsh naturalism of O'Flaherty's novel so much as he was seeking to make the audience understand and sympathize with a simple man driven by desperation to commit a heinous crime. The full squalor of Dublin's rotting slums may be obscured by night and fog and Ford's focus on the individual, but it is powerfully reflected in the misery and hopelessness of Gypo and his girlfriend, Katie Madden. Whatever criticism may be made of it, *The Informer* remains a haunting study of a soul in torment. Although it enjoyed only modest success at the box office, it won a host of awards.[14]

In 1936 Ford sought to repeat his artistic triumph with a screen version of Sean O'Casey's powerful play *The Plough and the Stars*. This time he failed. The studio insisted that he use Barbara Stanwyck in the lead role. Stanwyck was a good actress, but she was miscast in this part;[15] neither she nor Preston Foster, who played her husband, could match the acting of the supporting players from Dublin's famed Abbey Theater—among them Barry Fitzgerald, Arthur Shields, and F. J. McCormick. In O'Casey's play the heroine's husband dies in the 1916 insurrection against Britain, which forms the background of the story, causing her to go mad with grief. In the movie the lovers are reunited for one of Hollywood's typical happy endings. To make matters worse, RKO added some romantic scenes and dialogue clarifications, and recut the film to boost its box office appeal.[16] O'Casey's play has four acts; the film version runs only seventy-two minutes. Ford was wise to disclaim responsibility for the mutilated adaptation; it was a disaster. Yet he cannot fully escape responsibility for that disaster. There is some merit to one critic's charge that

The film's failure would seem to be largely the fault of Ford himself and his determination to turn O'Casey's ironic tragedy into a romantic and sentimental celebration of the struggle for Irish independence. Scenes from the play, shredded and theatrically performed, alternate with "heroic" IRA parades and stagey tableaux in the beleaguered Post Office. . . . The real lesson of *The Plough and the Stars* was that Ford's Irishness would always be a thing of romance and fantasy, and could never encompass the political and social realities of twentieth-century Ireland.[17]

Fifteen years passed before John Ford made another movie about Ireland. Since 1936, when he acquired the film rights, he had wanted to make a movie of Maurice Walsh's short story "The Quiet Man," and in 1951 he finally got the chance to do so. The result was to be the director's most personal statement about the land of his ancestors, a film that reflected the more mellow mood of a man nearing sixty who had been through two wars since *The Informer* and *The Plough and the Stars*. Ford called *The Quiet Man* (1952) his "first love story," and in a way he was right, for the love story is central to the movie and determines its course of action.[18] The "quiet man" is Sean Thornton (John Wayne), an exile returned to the land of his birth. Taken to America as a small boy, he has made his living in Pittsburgh's steel mills and the prize ring. After accidentally killing a man in the ring, Sean abandons prizefighting and returns to his native village of Innisfree, seeking the peace and happiness of his boyhood memories. Almost at once he falls in love with the fiery and beautiful Mary Kate Danaher (Maureen O'Hara) and, after overcoming the opposition of her bullying, oafish brother Red Will (Victor McLaglen), courts and weds her. But because Sean's friends have tricked Red Will into agreeing to the marriage, he refuses to pay Mary Kate's dowry. Without this symbol of her worth, Mary Kate cannot enjoy self-respect, and she refuses to be a real wife to Sean unless he obtains payment in full from her brother.[19] Still an outsider to the community, Sean cannot understand Mary Kate's obsession with the dowry. He cares nothing for the money, thinks Mary Kate's attitude mercenary and heartless, and will not confront Will to settle the issue. The traditions of the life Sean has yearned for have become the thorns on the rose. But, as Ford makes clear, Sean must learn to accept those traditions, or he can never find the happiness he seeks. In the end, he must break his vow never to fight again to save his marriage. Having forced Red Will to pay the dowry by threatening to return his sister to him, Sean (with Mary Kate's blessing) burns the money and thrashes Red Will in an uproarious marathon battle. Thus reconciled to the community, Sean finds happiness, and peace returns to Innisfree.

The Quiet Man is Ford's most reverential expression of his love for the land, community, and family. The love story is poignant, the comedy hilarious, and the color photography magnificent. It is entirely fitting that both Ford and his cinematographers won Oscars for their work, since direction and visual beauty are what most distinguish *The Quiet Man*.[20] For just over two hours, a master of composition and pacing unfolds his vision of Eden on the screen—a land of mist and sunshine, of cloud-dappled emerald fields, of cozy cottages, and quaint, endearing characters sustained by age-old values and rituals. The vision enchanted millions who saw it; it is as captivating as Oz or Brigadoon and almost as unreal.[21]

The village of Cong in County Mayo, where much of the movie was filmed, lies in one of the poorest as well as the most scenic parts of Ireland. Once filming was completed, this Potemkin village soon returned to its former shabby state. Notwithstanding the Irish Tourist Board's advertisements, there are few, if any, villages with homes as tidy and charming as those of Ford's Innisfree or with weather so agreeable. And how many are blessed with a parish priest at once as wise and as human as Father Peter Lonergan? Even the rural customs so prized by Ford were dying out when he made *The Quiet Man*. Yet none of this mattered to Ford, for he was not trying to portray social reality but to recreate a myth and reaffirm basic values. As Orson Welles reminded us, John Ford was a poet as well as a comedian.[22] In *The Quiet Man* he used his gifts to make "stage Irishmen" seem real, rocky fields fertile, and threatened values secure. George Moore's short story "Homesickness" (1903) gives a depressingly different picture of an exile's return to Erin. Moore, the realist, shows how things were; Ford, the romantic, shows how they should have been: and both men were great artists. In its warmth, humor, and visual beauty, *The Quiet Man* surpasses any other Ford movie. I suspect that is what he hoped for and that he was delighted by the picture's outstanding commercial success.[23]

Of *The Rising of the Moon* (1957), also filmed in Ireland, Ford recalled: "I made it just for fun and enjoyed it very much."[24] The movie consists of three unrelated segments: "The Majesty of the Law," "A Minute's Wait," and "1921." "A Minute's Wait," taken from a play by Michael J. McHugh, is a farcical sketch about the antic behavior of passengers, crew, and station attendants during a train's prolonged and (of course) unscheduled delay in a provincial station. The humor is overdone and soon becomes tiresome.[25] "1921" is an adaptation of Lady Gregory's famous one-act play *The Rising of the Moon*[26] about a hunted rebel and an Irish policeman with confused loyalties. It is a highly romantic and nostalgic version of Irish history. The same is true of "The Majesty of the Law," based on a short story by Frank O'Connor. By laying this sketch in the present (1957), Ford draws the contrast with the past even more sharply than in "1921." Dan O'Flaherty, a dignified relic of the old days, laments the passing of the old ways in Ireland, doomed by mass emigration and modern technology.[27] But his jeremiad rings hollow and raises questions about Ford's reverence for the past. If everything was so golden, why did millions of Irish flee overseas? Although it is easy to denounce modern materialism and a craze for novelty, a past that condemned so many to poverty and emigration leaves much more to be desired than to be regretted. The old ways offered no solution to Ireland's pressing economic problems; indeed, in some ways, they were part of those problems. Rather than lamenting vanishing tradition, O'Flaherty (and Ford) might better have lamented the vanishing Irish. The continuing violence in Northern Ireland is a reminder of just how destructive clinging to the old ways can sometimes be. *The Rising of the Moon* is not without flashes of insight and humor, but it lacks *The Quiet Man's* power of enchantment, and did poorly at the box office.

Ford's next Irish picture was to have been *Young Cassidy* (1965), based on part of Sean O'Casey's monumental autobiography *Mirror in My House*. After planning the project and filming a few scenes in Dublin, however, Ford fell ill and was replaced by director-cinematographer Jack Cardiff, who followed Ford's design for the picture fairly closely. The finished film is beautifully shot and scored,[28] but it is far from being a masterpiece. In tracing the theme of the importance of family and the role of the artist as social critic and outsider, *Young Cassidy* does present a picture of poverty and its victims that is, at times, grimly realistic, but it does not come to grips with the real Sean O'Casey or his ambivalent attitude toward the Irish nationalist movement. Except for the final scenes, Ford's version of the story would probably not have been much different.[29]

The canon of John Ford's Irish films would be incomplete if it did not include those about Irish Americans. Although he made only two films in which they occupy center stage, *The Long Gray Line* and *The Last Hurrah*, Ford often used Irish-American characters for comic relief, particularly with his post-World War II military movies. Almost invariably, these "darlin' boyos" are boozing, bragging brawlers, epitomized by Victor McLaglen. The most significant Irish presence occurs in *Fort Apache* (1948). In addition to the "stage Irish" types about whom James Agee complained,[30] the film features the O'Rourke family: Sergeant Major Michael O'Rourke (Ward Bond), his wife (Irene Rich), and their son Mickey (John Agar), a newly commissioned West Pointer. Ford uses the O'Rourkes not only to stress the important role that the Irish played in the United States Army, but also to examine the military caste system. In the Civil War O'Rourke senior had been a major in the 69th New York Infantry, an Irish-American regiment, and had won the Congressional Medal of Honor. But in a tiny peacetime army dominated by WASPs, there is virtually no room for his kind in the officer corps. (General Philip H. Sheridan and a handful of Irish Catholic junior officers were exceptions that proved this rule.) Mickey, however, is able to become "an officer and a gentleman" after his father's medal wins him admission to

West Point. The young man's aspirations soar even higher when he and his commanding officer's daughter fall in love, but here he runs afoul of the army's—and the nation's—caste system. His commander, Lieutenant Colonel Owen Thursday (Henry Fonda), an arrogant martinet, insists that union with Mickey is not "a proper or suitable marriage" for his daughter. And it is clear that the barrier that separates the two families is based as much on ethnicity as on Sergeant Major O'Rourke's status as an enlisted man.[31] Only the death of Thursday (who leads his command to destruction in an Indian ambush) makes it possible for the young people to marry and produce a son, Michael Thursday York O'Rourke, whose name and heritage are an example of the American "melting pot" in action. Such examples were rare, however, and the interplay between the O'Rourkes and the Thursdays reveals a good deal about military and social stratification a century ago.[32]

The Long Gray Line (1955) is a curious and unsatisfactory motion picture, very loosely based on the autobiography of Sergeant Martin Maher, who spent fifty years as an athletic trainer at West Point. Ford uses Maher's story to pay tribute to the nation's military traditions, which are a recurring theme in his work.[33] The trouble with *The Long Gray Line* is that Marty Maher (Tyrone Power) is an outsider to those traditions for most of the movie and his eventual assimilation is unconvincing. As an immigrant greenhorn, he doesn't want to join the army in the first place, wants to leave it through a good part of his career, and is a comic failure at the duties to which he is assigned. It is only after the deaths of his only child and, later, his wife (Maureen O'Hara) that Marty accepts the values of the military code and that the Corps of Cadets becomes his surrogate family. The reconciliation of outsider and community seems forced, however, and Marty's life seems sadly wasted. Ford's attempt to fuse the elitest traditions of the officer corps with the Irish-American experience doesn't work; the difference between them was simply too great, as Ford himself had shown in *Fort Apache*. Even its comic episodes are not very funny, and *The Long Gray Line* is more like a tragedy than anything else. Ironically, this uneven and unhappy film did very well commercially.[34]

Though much less successful at the box office, *The Last Hurrah* (1958) is a much better picture, thanks largely to the material on which it was based and the outstanding performance of its leading player, Spencer Tracy. Adroitly blending the warmth, humor, and nostalgia of Edwin O'Connor's best-selling novel about Boston politics and the final campaign of Mayor Frank Skeffington, a character loosely modeled on the famous Boston politico James Michael Curley (1874–1958), Ford composes a bittersweet elegy for a man and an age. The movie is filled with hilarious caricatures (Yankee as well as Irish), political shenanigans, community rituals, and echoes of the past out of which Skeffington and his people have come. Tracy's political chieftain is a complex and poignant figure who dwarfs the stereotypical figures surrounding him. If the reasons for his defeat by a young ninny remain somewhat obscure, that is unimportant, for the darkness and shadows that frame the major's radiant figure from the film's beginning have foretold that defeat. We mourn the passing of a titan and his age, but we do not question it. Few scenes in Ford's movies are as effective in conveying an idea and a mood as that in which Skeffington walks home alone in defeat while a victory parade marches past him in the opposite direction. Dying unrepentant and serene as the film ends, Tracy's Skeffington provides a memorable example of a favorite Fordian theme—"glory in defeat."[35]

The Last Hurrah is the only movie in which Ford tackled the Irish-American urban experience, and this seems a pity. Given his ability, experience, and the themes that so preoccupied him, he might have produced an enduring epic about the pioneers of the American ghetto. Still, he left a rich legacy of motion pictures, all of which owe something to his Irish heritage. Of *The Grapes of Wrath* (1940), which movingly portrayed the trials of an Okie family fleeing the Dust Bowl to seek the "Promised Land" in California, Ford recalled:

The whole thing appealed to me—being about simple people—and the story was similar to the famine in Ireland, when they threw the people off the land and left them wandering on the roads to starve. That may have had something to do with it—part of my Irish tradition—but I liked the idea of this family going out and trying to find their way in the world.[36]

In making *How Green Was My Valley* (1941), the story of the disintegration of a Welsh family and the mining community in which they live, Ford drew on memories of his own youth in Portland to evoke the mood he wanted. The Morgans were "just like my own family. Of course, they were Welsh, and we're Irish, but there was a great similarity."[37] Sara Allgood, who played Mrs. Morgan, looked like Ford's mother, and he made her act like his mother.[38] The Irish flavor imparted to the movie by Ford and Allgood was enhanced by the presence of Maureen O'Hara, Barry Fitzgerald, and Arthur Shields in the cast. When scriptwriter Philip Dunne complained about Ford's addition of an Irish drinking song to the picture, Ford rejoined: "Go on. The Welsh are the same as the Irish—a lot of goddamn micks and biddies, only Protestants."[39] And of his cavalry and Indian films, such as *Fort Apache*, Ford said:

More than having received Oscars, what counts for me is having been made a blood brother of various Indian nations. Perhaps it's my Irish atavism, my sense of reality, of the beauty of clans, in contrast to the modern world, the masses, the collective irresponsibility. Who better than an Irishman could understand the Indians, while still being stirred by the tales of the U.S. Cavalry? We were on both sides of the epic.[40]

While it is true that Ford's movies abound in stereotypes, these are usually entertaining, often endowed with distinguishing individual traits, and reflect even as they distort reality. Moreover, Ford offers rich character studies in his Irish films—among them, Gypo Nolan, Sean Thornton, Mary Kate Danaher, and Frank Skeffington. Although he was sometimes uncritical and unconvincing in his treatment of tradition, Ford said everything that could be said about its value. He conveyed a heightened sense of awareness about the vital importance of things like family, community, country, and ritual, depicting them in ways that touched the hearts of millions, making them laugh and cry and remember. Primarily a mythologizer, Ford was less interested in portraying reality than in affirming fundamental values, values derived from his Irish Catholic origins but at the same time transcending those origins. He could be and often was sentimental, vulgar, and chauvinistic, but he knew what people were made of, and his truth will endure, untarnished by changing political and social realities. As British film critic and director Lindsay Anderson said of John Ford almost forty years ago:

His work can be enjoyed by anyone, regardless of cultural level, who has retained his sensitivity and subscribes to values primarily humane. . . . Rich in phrasing, simple in structure, it is a style which expresses a sure, affirmative response to life—the equivalent to that Bibical prose which, today, it takes greatness of spirit to sustain.[41]

To Ireland, as to America, John Ford owed much; in both cases he more than repaid the debt.

War and Postwar, 1940–1960

That's one thing I've always admired about you Irish-Americans.
You carry your love of country like a flag, right out in the open.
It's a great quality.
President Franklin D. Roosevelt (Captain Jack Young) to George
M. Cohan (James Cagney) *Yankee Doodle Dandy* (1942)

YANKEE DOODLE DANDIES AT WAR

Long before World War II Irish Americans had proved their valor
and their devotion to their adopted country. Irish-Catholic immigrants had fought for the Union, enthusiastically and in large
numbers, and some of them remained in the army to take part in
the Indian wars of the late nineteenth century. On the eve of the
Spanish-American War, Joseph L. C. Clark glorified the patriotism
of his fellow Irish Americans with his popular poem, "The Fighting Race":

> "Well, here's to the Maine, and I'm sorry for Spain,"
> Said Kelly and Burke and Shea.

By the time of World War I, "the phrase 'fighting Irish,' which
had originated as a hostile label, became a proud boast, and the

image of the two-fisted, freckle-faced, redheaded Irishman who is twice as brave as anyone else has passed irretrievably into American folklore."[1]

Fighting Irishmen were featured in two of the best-known silent films about American warriors in 1917–1918. Tom O'Brien played John Gilbert's doughboy buddy Mike "Bull" O'Hara in *The Big Parade* (MGM, 1925), a tough bartender who became a tough noncom in the American Expeditionary Force. And Edmund Lowe played the irrepressible Sergeant Mickey Quirt, who was forever outwitting Victor McLaglen's explosive Captain Flagg in Raoul Walsh's ribald and action-packed *What Price Glory* (Fox, 1926), a popular adaptation of a successful play about U.S. Marines in France.

Movies about World War I were not popular during the Depression, when American reaction against involvement in that conflict was at its height. But beginning with *Confessions of a Nazi Spy* (Warner Bros., 1939), Hollywood began to turn out an increasing number of films attacking Hitler's Germany and warning Americans of the Nazi threat to democracy and individual liberty. Hollywood's contribution to the campaign for strengthening national defense was made partly through movies that recounted the heroism of American troops in World War I. *Sergeant York* (1941), the story of America's most decorated doughboy, was the most popular example of this type of propaganda, but it was preceded by *The Fighting 69th* (1940), a rousing account of New York's famous Irish-American regiment in training and combat.[2] As the 69th leaves for France, Father Duffy (Pat O'Brien) joins religion with patriotism as he prays for "the strength to keep them steadfast in faith, in decency and courage to the glory of God, their country, and their regiment, in the bad times to come."

Yankee Doodle Dandy (1942), an all-out effort to promote patriotism, went into production just as the United States entered World War II and was released six months later. This hagiographic biography of America's champion flagwaver, George M. Cohan, came along at just the right time. Shocked and angered by a series of defeats during the months following the Japanese attack on Pearl Harbor, Americans responded enthusiastically to the film as they turned again to subduing formidable foes "Over There." *Yankee Doodle Dandy* lifted the spirits of its dying subject and the nation he had glorified, confirming Americans' pride in their heritage and reinforcing their determination to win the war. It was as big a hit with the critics as with the audience. Reviewing the movie after its $5 million war bond premiere on May 29, 1942, Bosley Crowther wrote:

The picture magnificently matches the theatrical brilliance of Mr. Cohan's career, packed as it is with vigorous humor and honest sentiment. And the performance of Mr. Cagney as the one and original Song-and-Dance Man is an unbelievably faithful characterization and a piece of playing that glows with energy.[3]

Yankee Doodle Dandy won Cagney a richly deserved Oscar for his performance, as well as the New York Film Critics Award, and it remained his best and favorite role.[4]

During the war Hollywood lost access to most of its overseas markets and had to rely very heavily on domestic film rentals. However, the war brought full employment and high wages. With most commodities rationed and consumer goods in short supply, movies did a land office business. Domestic rentals for the major studios jumped from $193 million in 1939 to $332 million in 1946, and by war's end (1946) weekly attendance had again reached its 1930 peak of 90 million. During 1941–1942, about one out of four movies related in some way to the war effort. As the conflict continued, however, Hollywood made fewer (but better) war pictures, turning increasingly to the escapist fare its audience craved.[5]

The government wished to emphasize national unity during the war, and Hollywood was only too happy to oblige. Movie ship and airplane crews, as well as infantry squads and platoons, included stereotypical representatives of all major (and some minor) ethnic groups, who worked and fought together in a common cause. Since the "fighting Irishman" was a familiar national figure, he appeared in almost every war film and figured prominently in many. He might be a marine, like Private Joe Doyle (Robert Preston) in *Wake Island* (1942) or Sergeant "Hook" Malone (Lloyd Nolan) in *Guadalcanal Diary* (1943); a sailor, like Lieutenant (j.g.) "Rusty" Ryan (John Wayne) or "Boats" Mulcahy (Ward Bond) in John Ford's *They Were Expendable* (1945), or merchant seaman O'Hara (Alan Hale) in *Action in the North Atlantic* (1943); an airman, like B-17 pilot Captain Michael "Irish" Quincannon (John Ridgely) or bombardier Lieutenant McMartin (Arthur Kennedy) in Howard Hawks's *Air Force* (1943); an infantryman too tall for the air corps, like Private "Wingless" Murphy (Jack Reilly) in *The Story of G.I. Joe* (1945); or even an army nurse, like Lieutenant Joan O'Doul (Paulette Goddard) in *So Proudly We Hail* (1943). In *The Purple Heart* (1944), a gripping account of the show trial of downed B-25 fliers who had participated in the April 1942 air raid on Japan, Lieutenant Peter Vincent is the quick-tempered member of the crew. To remove any doubts about his ethnic origins, Vincent is played by Don "Red" Barry, a Cagney-type actor in looks and manner. In the same film, Sergeant Jan Skvoznik is played by Kevin O'Shea, and the crew's bomber was named "Mrs. Murphy." And so it went.

For those who preferred depiction of real-life Irish heroes, there was the character based on Colonel Paddy Ryan, the tireless advocate of precision bombing, played by Pat O'Brien in *Bombardier* (1943). (O'Brien also appeared as Frank Cavanaugh, the famous college football coach and World War I hero, in *The Iron Major* [1943].) Or Father Ignatius Donnelly (Notre Dame, '28), a navy chaplain portrayed by Preston Foster in *Guadalcanal Diary*. Most poignantly, there were the Sullivans, five brothers from Waterloo, Iowa, all killed when their ship, the cruiser *Juneau*, was sunk off Guadalcanal. *The Sullivans* (1944, retitled *The Fighting Sullivans*) is a heartrending story that traces the brothers' lives before the war, with only the final few minutes devoted to their deaths and the impact of the news on their family. In recreating their boyhood scrapes and escapades, the movie presents a picture of a close-knit family, rich in love and humor, and Irish American through and through. Thomas Mitchell was excellent as the boys' father, as was Eddie Ryan as the youngest brother, Al, who gets the most attention in the film. Following the Sullivans' death, the navy prohibited brothers from serving on the same ship and named a destroyer for them. Their parents observed production of the movie in Hollywood and attended its premiere in New York City, selling war bonds on that occasion.[6] When the war finally ended, it turned out that the most decorated American serviceman was a youthful Texas sharecropper-turned-infantryman, whose name was Audie Murphy. He won a battlefield commission and the Congressional Medal of Honor, as well as many other decorations. His heroic story was later filmed as *To Hell and Back* (1955), with Murphy, who became an actor after the war, playing himself.

On the home front, Spencer Tracy as reporter Steven O'Malley battled fascism, American-style, in *Keeper of the Flame* (1943), while Humphrey Bogart as racketeer "Gloves" Donahue outwitted Nazi saboteurs in *All Through the Night* (1942). In Preston Sturges' *Sullivan's Travels*, (1941), acclaimed movie director John L. Sullivan (Joel McCrea) becomes obsessed with the idea of making a serious statement about the meaning of life, only to learn by painful experience that laughter is the best medicine for the human condition. Leo McCarey delivered the same message with resounding success in *Going My Way*, the big hit of 1944.[7] *Sweet Rosie O'Grady* (1943) and *When Irish Eyes Are Smiling* (1944) were period musicals that traded on the popularity of durable Irish-American songs.

Aside from war movies and *Going My Way*, the Irish were featured most prominently in two period dramas, *The Valley of Decision* (1945) and *A Tree Grows in Brooklyn* (1945). The former is set in Pittsburgh in the 1870s when it was rapidly becoming the steel-making capital of the world. In admittedly cautious fashion, the film explores the relations of capital and labor, of WASP overlords and Irish servants in this turbulent period of American history. County Down's own Greer Garson, who won an Oscar for her portrayal of *Mrs. Miniver* (1942), plays Mary Rafferty, a poor Catholic girl whose embittered father, Pat (Lionel Barrymore), has long since been crippled by an accident in the Scotts' steel mill. Mary becomes a maid in the Scott household and falls in love with the eldest son, Paul (Gregory Peck). As might be expected, however, the path of true love is far from smooth, and it takes almost fifteen years before Mary and Paul are finally united. In the meantime, a strike for union recognition by the Irish millhands brings about the deaths of both Scott Senior (Donald Crisp) and Pat Rafferty, as well as Mary's disappointed suitor, Jim Brennan (Preston Foster). The story is not much more than a glossy soap opera, but the cast is first rate, and the movie does attempt to show, however timidly, the discrimination suffered by the Irish at the hands of the ruling WASPs. Jim Brennan, the union leader, is shown to be a reasonable man, and one can well understand Pat Rafferty's hatred of the Scotts, even if one knows that hatred is not the answer. In resolving ethnic and class differences through romance, MGM provides the usual "Pat" answer to problems. Even so, *The Valley of Decision* was fairly bold stuff for a studio whose main claims to fame were the "Andy Hardy" movies, lavish musicals, and *The Wizard of Oz*.

A more realistic portrayal of the trials of Irish immigrants is given in 20th Century-Fox's *A Tree Grows In Brooklyn*, based on Betty Smith's popular novel about her childhood in the early 1900s. This was director Elia Kazan's first film, and it remains the best about the pioneers of the urban ghetto, less praised and powerful than his later *On the Waterfront*, but also less melodramatic and more honest. Even with the glosses mandated by the Production Code Administration and with studio sets, *A Tree Grows in Brooklyn* is a moving account of tenement life. The members of the Nolan family—Johnny (James Dunn), his German-American wife Katie (Dorothy McGuire), and their two children, Francie and Neely—as well as those with whom they come in contact are shown as fully rounded individuals, not just stereotypes. The Nolans' poverty, drudgery, and desperation, their pain, love, and dreams are vividly depicted on the screen. Although all the performances are very good, acting honors belong to James Dunn for his superb portrayal of the feckless alcoholic Johnny Nolan, the role that won him an Oscar. A singing waiter with a longer wait between jobs than drinks, Johnny is a gentle and charming self-deceiver who lives on the love of his family and his dream of theatrical discovery. After losing his wife's faith (but not her love) and learning that a new baby is on the way, Johnny seeks to redeem himself by finding a steady job that will support his family. He finally lands one, following an exhausting search in the dead of winter, only to perish of exposure and pneumonia. We do not witness his frenzied hunt for work or his collapse, but we feel them keenly in Officer McShane's (Lloyd Nolan) report to Katie, especially in the words, "he hadn't been drinkin', Ma'am." And we share the widow's grief as she pleads with the medical examiner not to list alcoholism as a contributory cause of death. By the end of the film, it is clear that things are at last looking up for Katie and her brood, but it is also clear that they will never forget Johnny, and we understand why this is so. Johnny may have lived in the gutter, but he was looking at the stars, and his vision warmed the hearts of all who knew him.

In a way, the very depiction of the poverty and misery suffered by the Irish in films like *The Valley of Decision* and *A Tree Grows in Brooklyn* signaled their tremendous progress in America. Now that the Irish had truly arrived and left their tragic past behind, it was safe to show that past, for to most Irish and other Americans it had ceased to matter. Historian Richard Polenberg is correct when he says of wartime America: "The war, while not erasing all sense of ethnic distinctiveness, surely softened it, as older immigrant communities and the institutions that served them lost strength."[8]

During the war years a new crop of Irish performers, some of whom proved very durable, rose to prominence on the silver screen. Maureen O'Hara's ravishing beauty, Greer Garson's quiet dignity and warmth, Geraldine Fitzgerald's almost neurotic intensity, and Dorothy McGuire's appealing shyness made them stars in short order, although Fitzgerald's battles with Warners for better roles shortened her career as a leading lady. Less durable or successful, but considered promising newcomers during the forties were Janet Blair (Lafferty), Barbara Hale, Ann Blyth, Maggie Hayes, Nancy Kelly, Martha O'Driscoll, Sally Forrest (Feeney), Peggy Ryan, and Sheila Ryan (McLaughlin). Margaret O'Brien's ability to weep at the drop of a hankerchief helped make her Shirley Temple's successor as the movies' reigning child star.

The wartime shortage of leading men assisted the careers of Barry Sullivan (Patrick Barry), Stephen (Horace) McNally, and Michael O'Shea as dramatic actors. It did more for Eugene Curran Kelly, whose success in Rodgers and Hart's *Pal Joey* took him from Broadway to Hollywood, where he costarred with Judy Garland in *For Me and My Gal* (1942), a nostalgic musical of the World War I era. Kelly's charm and grace in that picture launched him on a movie career that would make him almost a legend in the 1950s. Robert Ryan and Arthur Kennedy were also products of the stage, and both made their mark as supporting actors in films before wartime military service interrupted their work. When they resumed acting after the war, Ryan and Kennedy would enjoy long and rewarding careers on stage and screen. Neither man ever became a "star" in the usually accepted meaning of that term. But they played a variety of challenging parts brilliantly in the postwar period, proving that they were two of the most talented actors America has ever produced.

McCARTHYISM AND McCAREYISM

In the decade and a half following World War II, the Irish continued the steady progress they had made in the Roosevelt era. Organized labor consolidated the gains made during the New Deal and war years, whereas the GI Bill of Rights (1944) enabled Irish Americans as well as other veterans to attend college in large numbers. Except in the biggest cities, Irish neighborhoods had all but disappeared by the 1950s, as the Irish moved in ever increasing numbers from the inner cities to the suburbs. During this period first- and second-generation Irish Americans were rapidly disappearing (except for a trickle of immigrants), and later generations were becoming the representatives of this ethnic group.[9]

The motion picture industry did not fare so well in the postwar years; indeed, it faced serious financial and political problems. The television industry grew rapidly, and by the early 1950s television viewing had become America's major leisure-time activity. Between 1946 and 1957, weekly movie attendance fell by half, from 90 to 45 million, even though the total population increased by 30 million during those years. Even with higher ticket prices, box office receipts fell by 30 percent, 1946–1957, and the combined profits of the ten biggest movie companies declined by 74 percent, 1946–1956. The failure to regain foreign markets because of the Cold War, import restrictions imposed by countries short of dollars, and support by these countries for domestic film industries were other blows to Hollywood in the postwar period. The federal government's successful antitrust suit against the movie companies, which forced divestiture of their theater chains, also had a serious initial impact. The loss of assured marketing outlets was an important factor in the major studios' decision to cut back production, an action that reduced the number of actors under contract by two-thirds, 1947–1956, and cut the total work force from 24,000 in 1946 to about 13,000 in 1956.[10]

Separation of exhibition from production and distribution also affected the content of motion pictures. Since the five major studios no longer owned first-run theaters, they could not enforce the PCA's restrictions. The PCA suffered another serious blow when the U.S. Supreme Court, reversing its 1915 decision, extended the protection of the First Amendment to movies in 1952, giving them much greater freedom of expression and choice of subject matter. An influx of foreign films, which treated sexual matters much more frankly than Hollywood, further weakened the Production Code, as did the increasing number of American movies filmed abroad, far from PCA supervision. With postwar developments thus undermining the power of the PCA and the Legion of Decency, developments that included and partly reflected the public's somewhat more permissive sexual attitudes, the censors were forced onto the defensive. The fact that television had replaced movies as the dominant entertainment medium does much to explain the growing tolerance for greater freedom of content in motion pictures. As movies became less popular and influential, television attracted most of the moral surveillance once reserved for them. Thus relaxation of censorship and greater realism in filmmaking was one positive result of the movies' declining fortunes.[11]

Hollywood's first reaction to television was to ignore it, hoping that it would prove no more than a passing fad. When it demonstrated growing and enduring popularity, movies fought back with wide screens, color, and 3-D to reclaim their lost audiences. When none of the innovations halted the decline, the industry belatedly decided to cooperate with television, selling the new medium its huge library of feature films, producing programs (and later movies) for TV, merging studios with TV companies, and buying TV stations. By 1960 it was clear that motion pictures had permanently lost their primacy to television, but it was equally clear that they were coming to terms with the new order of things.[12]

Aggravating Hollywood's postwar problems was a "Red scare," which was both a cause and an effect of the nation's Cold War with the Soviet Union and its allies. Anti-Communist hysteria reached its peak during the Korean War (1950–1953), when it was labeled "McCarthyism," after its chief fomenter, Wisconsin's Republican Senator Joseph R. McCarthy. Before McCarthy finally overreached himself and was censured by the Senate in 1954, the witch hunt he led had done the nation incalculable harm, dividing it deeply and ruining the lives of many innocent people smeared by McCarthy and his impassioned supporters. The witch hunt actually began in Hollywood before it did anywhere else—before the Hiss and Rosenberg espionage cases, the Communist coup in Czechoslovakia, the Soviet blockade of West Berlin, the Communist victory in the Chinese civil war, or the invasion of South Korea by the Communist North Koreans.

In 1947, after an interlude of seven years, the U.S. House of Representatives Committee on Un-American Activities (HUAC) resumed its investigation of communism in the motion picture industry. The conservatives who controlled the Eightieth Congress were bitter enemies of Franklin D. Roosevelt and the New Deal, who sought to discredit the dead president and his programs. They selected Hollywood as their primary target because of the publicity this would give HUAC members and their anti-Communist, antiradical, antiliberal crusade. With great fanfare, the committee sought to prove that Communists had infiltrated the movie industry, particularly the Screen Writers Guild, that they and their sympathizers had spread subversive propaganda through the movies, and that FDR had pressured the studios to make pro-Soviet films during the war. "Friendly witnesses," including Leo McCarey and George Murphy, lent support to the committee's charges of Communist subversion. Ten "unfriendly witnesses"—seven screenwriters, two directors, and a producer (none Irish)—questioned as to their membership in the Communist party truculently defied the committee, generating much unfavorable publicity by their arrogant manner and evasive responses.

The so-called Hollywood Ten were quickly cited for contempt of Congress, tried, and convicted. Fined $1,000 each and sentenced to a year in federal prison, the ten were "blacklisted" (denied employment) by the motion picture industry. Although HUAC held further hearings (1951–1953) and (with evidence provided by the FBI) turned up a number of Communist party members in the movie industry, it produced no convincing evidence that the Communists had successfully infiltrated the industry, that the movies were spreading Communist propaganda, or that the Roosevelt Administration had played a major role in the studios' decision to make films (only a handful) favorably depicting our Russian ally during World War II. HUAC had, however, gotten the limelight with its investigation of Hollywood's "Reds," and it had destroyed the careers and lives of many people who were guilty of nothing more than membership in the Communist party when it was a legal organization, often a membership that was brief and had long since lapsed. Moreover, the investigation had panicked the studio heads, put liberals on the defensive, and badly damaged the motion picture industry.

In the wake of hostile public reaction to the "Hollywood Ten's" appearance before HUAC, the initial resistance of the studio heads to the inquisition collapsed. In late November 1947 fifty leading movie executives met in New York City. After a two-day session, they issued a statement denouncing the "Hollywood Ten" for their uncooperative attitude with HUAC and suspending them without pay. The executives pledged that they would not knowingly employ a Communist and invited the various screen guilds to help weed out subversives from the industry. The result of this surrender was a blacklist, which was used to deny employment to anyone accused of being a "subversive" by right-wing groups inside and outside the motion picture industry. This blacklist remained in force until the early 1960s. Those on it who were admitted Communist party members could clear themselves only by public confession and recantation before HUAC. This ritual included "naming names" of former Communist associates. Those who refused to cooperate with HUAC and its allied anti-Communist lobbies were denied employment. Non-Communists, unable to "name names" of Communist party members for HUAC, often found it difficult to clear themselves of charges made against them. In its panic, "Hollywood had completely capitulated to the Red Scare, its perpetrators, and the right-wing guardians who had mobilized to cleanse the industry of undesirables. It could then add moral enfeeblement to its list of ailments." [13]

It should be noted that this capitulation was not due primarily to fear of Communist subversion but to fear of boycott and picketing by superpatriotic organizations like the American Legion. Such actions did occur from time to time, as numerous pressure groups joined HUAC in its assault on Hollywood. As was the case with censorship in the 1930s, it was the threat of an economic boycott that created and maintained the blacklist. [14]

Throughout the nation as in Hollywood, Irish Americans were divided by the Red scare. Although Catholics formed only a minority of Senator McCarthy's supporters, he did have more Catholic adherents than critics, including many Irish Catholics. In January 1954 McCarthy was at the peak of his power, enjoying the support of 58 percent of Catholics and 49 percent of Protestants, according to a Gallup poll. In September 1954, following the televised Army-McCarthy hearings, which badly damaged the senator's image, his support among Protestants had declined sharply, to 23 percent, whereas 40 percent of Catholics still supported him. Whatever their attitude toward Senator McCarthy, the increasing prosperity of Irish Catholics and the hostility of their church toward communism did draw a growing number of them toward political conservatism in the 1950s, even into the Republican party.[15]

The reasons for Catholic support of Senator McCarthy are not hard to understand, quite apart from the fact that McCarthy himself was a Catholic (of Irish-German extraction). The United States had ended World War II as the most powerful nation on earth; yet a scant five years later, it was on the defensive everywhere, with communism a growing threat abroad and, apparently, even at home. Perhaps McCarthy was right when he said that only treason could account for Communist victories and American setbacks in the Cold War, and perhaps the traitors were WASP intellectuals like Alger Hiss, members of the nation's highly privileged elite. Certainly McCarthy was fighting against an atheistic creed that persecuted the Catholic church in Eastern Europe, and just as certainly his enemies in the United States were political and intellectual leaders of a kind long notorious for their anti-Catholicism (and anti-Irishness), even if their opposition was now based on an ideology of secular liberalism rather than militant Protestantism. Many priests praised McCarthy, and only one bishop openly condemned him. It was not difficult to believe that McCarthy's anti-Communist and anti-nativist campaign was just what was needed by the Irish and other ethnic minorities to defeat the forces of liberal relativism, take power, and defeat communism at home and abroad.

At best, the Irish position at this time rested on profoundly responsible religious convictions. At its worst, Irish anti-Communism was not directed at Communism at all. From start to finish, McCarthy got his largest response from the New York Irish when he attacked the institutions of the white Anglo-Saxon Protestant establishment. It was Harvard University and the State Department and the United States Army that seemed to be subverting the country.[16]

And, "In the era of security clearances, to be an Irish Catholic became *prima facie* evidence of loyalty. Harvard men were to be checked; Fordham men would do the checking."[17]

In Hollywood as well as elsewhere the lines were sharply drawn during the Red scare. Ronald Reagan, beginning an odyssey that would take him from ultraliberalism to ultraconservatism, reacted strongly to what he perceived as Communist attempts at manipulation and intimidation in the Screen Actors Guild. As president of the Guild (1947–1952), Reagan helped enforce the blacklist, although continuing to deny its existence. Also prominent in the anti-Red crusade were George Murphy, Leo McCarey, and writer-producer James Kevin McGuinness, an influential member of the arch-conservative Motion Picture Alliance for the Preservation of American Ideals. The most outspoken Irish opponent of the congressional inquisition and the ensuing blacklist was screenwriter Philip Dunne, seconded by fellow liberals Robert Ryan and Gene Kelly. Three-term president of the Screen Writers Guild (1944–1947) Emmet Lavery, Catholic, a Democrat, and moderately liberal, tried to steer a middle course in the controversy, denouncing both HUAC's tactics and Communist members of the SWG, a course of action that left him open to attacks from both right and left. Crusty John Ford, champion of traditional American values and now a superpatriot, was still rebel enough openly to denounce HUAC's methods at least twice in 1947. And in 1950 Ford's opposition helped to defeat an attempt by Cecil B. DeMille and likeminded reactionaries to purge the Screen Directors Guild of all those who disagreed with their brand of ultraconservatism.[18] Not surprisingly under the circumstances, most members of the motion picture community, Irish as well as non-Irish, did their best to remain aloof from the struggle, and kept quiet.

The wave of political repression and the national mood of conformity that followed it were reflected in the movies of the 1950s. During and just after the war, Hollywood produced an increasing number of films that addressed social problems with a fair amount of realism. These movies dealt with such issues as American fascism, racism, anti-Semitism, alcoholism, mental illness, and the readjustment of veterans to civilian life. Such subjects were much too controversial for a Hollywood under siege by militant right-wing organizations. Social problem films all but disappeared during the early fifties, to be replaced by anti-Communist polemics and escapist fare so devoid of social content as to offend no one.

Noteworthy among the spate of anti-Red films were *Big Jim McLain* (1952) and *My Son John* (1952). The former is a piece of crude, flag-waving propaganda sugared with romance and religion. The movie announced that it was based on HUAC files and made with HUAC cooperation. John Wayne is the Irish-American hero, a HUAC investigator who breaks up a Communist sabotage ring in Hawaii. Instead of handing over the culprits to the courts for trial, however, McLain brings them before HUAC, where they escape punishment by taking the Fifth Amendment against self-incrimination. This is a travesty of fact, not of our system of justice. But such misrepresentation enables McLain to assert that a constitution meant to protect "honest, decent citizens" should not serve to shield those who seek to destroy it. Denying to others the rights we claim for ourselves, betraying liberty while posing as its guardians—these things are the essence of McCarthyism.

Like the spurious "110 percent Americanism" of *Big Jim McLain,* Leo McCarey's *My Son John* is a sad reminder of a time when a great many Americans were convinced that a threat that was primarily external and military was internal and ideological. John Jefferson (Robert Walker) is an arrogant pseudo-intellectual of Irish Catholic stock who joins the Communist party, betrays his family, his religion, and his country, and is eventually murdered by his former comrades as the FBI closes in on him. His mother and father (Helen Hayes and Dean Jagger) represent the traditional "bourgeois" values that John scorns. Although he is a schoolteacher himself, Mr. Jefferson distrusts his son's university education. Ignorant and intolerant, he makes no effort to present logical arguments against what he opposes but takes refuge in patriotic and Biblical cliches, raising his fists as well as his voice against his son in a fit of drunken anger. John's mother is menopausal and anxiety-ridden, torn between her religion and her mother love for an errant son. Despite its talented cast, the film is terrible.

An anti-Communist polemic, *My Son John* neither educates nor entertains. As reviewer Bosley Crowther pointed out, it "is a picture so strongly dedicated to the purpose of the American anti-Communist purge that it seethes with the sort of emotionalism and illogic that is characteristic of so much thinking these days."[19] Athough it failed at the box office as well as with the critics, the film did have its fans. It was named one of the ten best films of 1952 by the National Board of Review, and Leo McCarey's original story was nominated for (although it did not win) an Academy Award.[20]

The one really good film to come out of the Red scare of the fifties was Elia Kazan's *On the Waterfront* (1954), a hard-hitting exposé of corruption and murder on the Hoboken (New Jersey) docks. Prodded by social activist Father Barry (Karl Malden) and girlfriend Edie Doyle (Eva Marie Saint), and enraged by the murder of his brother Charley (Rod Steiger), longshoreman Terry Malloy (Marlon Brando) informs on a crooked union boss (Lee J. Cobb) to the state crime commission. By breaking the waterfront code of "D and D" (deaf and dumb), Malloy redeems himself from being an unwitting tool of the boss and frees his fellow longshoremen from the clutches of the hoodlums. He even attains a kind of martyrdom by suffering a vicious beating at the hands of the boss's gang. The story is told in quasi-documentary fashion, and with its brilliant direction, acting, script, cinematography, and musical score, *On the Waterfront* is compelling drama. A box office smash, the film won most of the major awards in 1954–1955, including Oscars for best picture, best director, best actor, and best story and screenplay. The subtext of this indictment of wrong-doing and those who allow it to continue through misguided notions of loyalty is the bitter argument between those who "named names" for HUAC and those who refused to do so over who was right. Kazan and screenwriter Budd Schulberg were among the former, and they used *On the Waterfront* to justify their informing, an action they asserted served the nation's welfare and one based on principle rather than mere opportunism.[21] Needless to say, those who did not "name names" rejected this contention, pointing out important differences between Terry Malloy's case and that of the HUAC informers. *On the Waterfront* would not be the only movie to address this highly controversial issue, although none taking an opposing point of view could be made while the blacklist was still in effect.[22]

Of course, the Irish were not limited to movies that dealt directly or indirectly with communism in the years between 1945 and 1960. They appeared in all the film genres and in many different kinds of roles, including the ones in the John Ford films already mentioned. The *Yankee Doodle Dandy* tradition continued with *My Wild Irish Rose* (1947), a largely fictionalized biography of the Irish-American troubador Chauncey Olcott (Dennis Morgan), and *The Seven Little Foys* (1955), starring Bob Hope as Eddie Foy and featuring James Cagney in a cameo role as George M. Cohan. Other movies about Irish vaudeville troupers included *The Merry Monahans* (1944), *Patrick the Great* (1945), *Give My Regards to Broadway* (1948), and *There's No Business Like Show Business* (1954). The first two starred the talented young dancer Donald O'Connor, the last two starred the equally talented song-and-dance man Dan Dailey, supported by O'Connor in *Show Business*. *The Fabulous Dorseys* (1947) provided first-rate musical accompaniment for the childish feuding of the two popular bandleader brothers—Jimmy and Tommy Dorsey. The brothers played themselves, with Sara Allgood and Arthur Shields as their loving and long-suffering parents.

For those who liked comedies, even mediocre ones, there was Tyrone Power in *The Luck of the Irish* (1948); Bing Crosby, Barry Fitzgerald, and Ann Blyth in *Top o' the Morning* (1949); and Sean Connery in Walt Disney's *Darby O'Gill and the Little People* (1959). For historical adventure fans, there were Stephen Fox (Rex Harrison) and Mike Farrell (Victor McLaglen) in *The Foxes of Harrow* (1947), a turgid drama set in antebellum Louisiana, with lovely Maureen O'Hara as the Creole romantic interest. For derring-do in Ould Ireland, one could go see *The Fighting O'Flynn* (1949), featuring J. M. Kerrigan and Arthur Shields in support of Douglas Fairbanks, Jr. For boxing fans, there was *The Great John L.* (1945), a Bing Crosby production with Greg McClure as John L. Sullivan, and *Champion* (1949), with Kirk Douglas as the ruthless fighter Midge Kelly and Arthur Kennedy as his lame brother Connie.

Manhattan in the 1920s was the setting of *Beau James* (1957), the story of Mayor Jimmy Walker (Bob Hope), and Chicago's South Side of *Studs Lonigan* (1960), an unsuccessful adaptation of James T. Farrell's literary work. *The Catered Affair* (1956) purported to be a realistic view of Irish family life in the contemporary Bronx, but it was only partially redeemed by Barry Fitzgerald's performance as "Uncle Jack." Rebellion in Ireland was the subject of *Captain Lightfoot* (1955) and, in a much more somber vein, of *Shake Hands with the Devil* (1959) and *The Night Fighters* (1960, a British production starring Robert Mitchum). All three of these movies were filmed in Ireland (the first in glorious color) and all employed native Irish actors in secondary roles. *The Night Fighters,* like other British films dealing with the subject, offered a highly critical view of the Irish Republican Army and its attempts to undo partition.

Whereas it would be both impossible and pointless to list all the Irish characters in movies made between 1945 and 1960 (or in any other period, for that matter), a random sample indicates their variety and ubiquity. Spencer Tracy as the doomed, alcoholic lawyer James P. Curtayne in *The People Against O'Hara* (1951), as the wily sports promoter Mike Conovan in *Pat and Mike* (1952), and as the tyrannical cattle baron Matt Devereaux in *Broken Lance* (1954). Alan Ladd as racetrack gambler *Salty O'Rourke* (1945) and U.S. Air Force ace and test pilot Captain Joseph McConnell in *The McConnell Story* (1955). "Good-bad girls" Eloise "Honeybear" Kelly (Ava Gardner) in *Mogambo* (1953) and Mae Doyle (Barbara Stanwyck) in *Clash by Night* (1952). Kirk Douglas as weak-willed Walter O'Neill, Barbara Stanwyck's husband, in *The Strange Love of Martha Ivers* (1946) and as Jim Fallon, the ruthless but redeemable frontier timber baron in *The Big Trees* (1952). Arthur O'Connell as Parnell Emmet McCarthy, James Stewart's rumpled legal associate in *Anatomy of a Murder* (1959); Gary Cooper's lecherous tycoon Frank Flanagan in *Love in the Afternoon* (1957); Brian Keith's diamond-in-the-rough contractor Mike Flanagan in *The Young Philadelphians* (1959); Tom Tully's slick politician Mike Slattery in *Ten North Frederick* (1958); Frank Morgan's boisterous firechief in *The Key to the City* (1949); and Pat O'Brien's "Gramp" in that forgotten plea for brotherhood, *The Boy with Green Hair* (1948). The Oscar-winning performances of Mercedes McCambridge as Sadie Burke, the hard-asnails political advisor in *All the King's Men* (1949), and Claire Trevor as Gay Dawn (Maggie Mooney), gangster Edward G. Robinson's castoff alcoholic mistress in *Key Largo* (1948). Deborah Kerr as the courageous Irish nun in *Heaven Knows, Mr. Allison* (1957), a role that gained her an Oscar nomination. In *Portrait of Jennie* (1948), the philosophical cabbie Gus (David Wayne) and the excitable bar-and-grill owner Moore (Albert Sharpe), with his shouts of "Up the rebels!" and his mural of Michael Collins leading the IRA into battle. The uproarious Finney family (Connie Gilchrist, Linda Darnell, and Barbara Lawrence) and their equally uproarious pal Sadie Dugan (Thelma Ritter) in *A Letter to Three Wives* (1949). The pugnacious cowboy in the billycock hat (Ray Hyke) in *Red River* (1948); the fiery frontier colleen Vermillion O'Toole (Ann Sheridan) in *Take Me to Town* (1953); and Sergeant Major Duffy (Jay C. Flippen) in *Two Flags West* (1950). World War II navy flier J. J. McCann (Ray Walston) in *Kiss Them for Me* (1957); navy beachmaster Mike O'Bannion (Charles McGraw) in *Away All Boats* (1957); OSS agent Bob Sharkey (James Cagney) in *13 Rue Madeleine* (1947); and the outrageous helicopter pilot Mike Forney (Mickey Rooney) in the Korean War drama, *The Bridges at Toko-Ri* (1955). Two ex-GIs (both played by Gene Kelly), the expatriate painter Jerry Mulligan in *An American in Paris* (1951) and Ted Riley, the slightly shady but ultimately honest small-time operator, in *It's Always Fair Weather* (1955). Turn-of-the-century baseball players-cum-vaudevillians Eddie O'Brien and Dennis Ryan (Gene Kelly and Frank Sinatra) in *Take Me Out to the Ball Game* (1949). Dixieland cornet player Pete Kelly (Jack Webb) confronting gangster Fran McCarg (Edmond O'Brien) in Jazz Age Kansas City in *Pete Kelly's Blues* (1955). Insurance investigator Jim Reardon (Edmond O'Brien) tracking down femme fatale Kitty Collins (Ava Gardner) in *The Killers* (1946). Orson Welles' romantic adventurer Michael O'Hara in *The Lady from Shanghai* (1948) and his corrupt, obese bordertown detective, Hank Quinlan, in *Touch of Evil* (1958). The Murphys in the outdated and unsuccessful remake of *Abie's Irish Rose* (1946), and Mike Dillon (Dana Andrews), an opportunist who embraces Israel's cause in the much more timely *Sword in the Desert* (1948). Last but by no means least, there is that old standby the Irish cop, depicted most memorably in the postwar era as Lieutenant Finley (Robert

Young) in *Crossfire* (1947). After trapping and killing an anti-Semitic murderer (masterfully played by Robert Ryan), Finley sums up the end result of bigotry by recalling the murder of his immigrant grandfather by nativist bullies.

In post–World War II movies the Irish are everywhere, but they often go unnoticed, because by this time their presence is simply taken for granted as part of the scene. The old stereotypes still exist, but in most cases they have been so refined that they are hard to recognize. The distinctive brogue, dress, and behavior have been largely discarded; only the names have not been changed. For good and ill, the Irish have moved into the mainstream.

GRACE KELLY AND GENE KELLY: "ALL AMERICANS"

Two performers named Kelly—Grace and Gene—personify Irish assimilation in the movies of the 1950s. Grace Kelly, the daughter of a highly successful, self-made Philadelphia contractor and a former cover girl, made only eleven films between 1951 and 1956 before retiring from the screen to become princess of Monaco (where she lived until her tragic death in a car accident in 1982). But in that time she won an Oscar, became director Alfred Hitchcock's favorite leading lady, and established herself as the national symbol of beauty and class. Her cool exterior and obvious good breeding combined with her blond loveliness and the suggestion of passions held carefully in check made her the reigning goddess of refined sex. The daughter of an Irish bricklayer became the American ideal: the dreamgirl of young, upward-bound males who yearned for the finer things of life, and a female idol as well, for what more could any American girl aspire to in that prefeminist age than to become a genuine princess. In both real life and reel life, Grace Kelly fulfilled the promise of American life.

If Grace Kelly was the American dreamgirl, Gene Kelly was the All-American boy. His kind of dancing—exuberant, athletic, full of freshness and vitality—made him the symbol of postwar America—youthful, confident, resourceful, bursting with energy and optimism. During his career, Kelly played many straight dramatic roles (and several different nationalities). He was also a competent film director. But it is as a dancer and choreographer that Gene

Kelly will be remembered, especially for his work in four innovative MGM musicals that won widespread critical and popular acclaim: *On the Town* (1949), *An American in Paris* (1951), *Singin' in the Rain* (1952), and *It's Always Fair Weather* (1955). In these movies Kelly demonstrated his versatility as a dancer and his creativity as a choreographer. Irrepressible and irresistible, he tripped the light fantastic with a twinkle in his eyes and a highly infectious grin. Gene Kelly personified the mood of an America that had emerged triumphant and almost unscathed from World War II, an America that seemed sure there was no problem it could not solve, no obstacle it could not overcome. He was part of *The Best Years of Our Lives,* a phrase that represented much more than the title of the award-winning 1946 movie classic about veterans' readjustment to civilian life. That era ended as the Cold War dragged on and setbacks gradually sapped American confidence. But while it lasted, Kelly embodied its spirit. He often played an Irish American in his movies, but he was always an All-American. In 1952, the year that *An American in Paris* won the Academy Award for best picture (of 1951), Kelly was given an honorary Oscar "in appreciation of his versatility as an actor, singer, director, and dancer, and specifically for his brilliant achievements in the art of choreography on film." In 1985 Kelly received the American Film Institute's Life Achievement Award, an acknowledgment that his contributions to motion pictures were comparable to those of two earlier recipients of the award—John Ford and James Cagney (1973 and 1974).[23]

Although their impact was not so great as that of the two Kellys, there were other Irish performers who demonstrated their talent in the postwar era. Dan Dailey and Donald O'Connor proved themselves to be accomplished dancers and competent actors. The former costarred with Gene Kelly in *It's Always Fair Weather;* the latter "stopped the show" with his "Make 'Em Laugh" number in *Singin' in the Rain.* Richard Egan and Stephen Boyd (Billy Millar from Belfast) played leads and second leads in a variety of films. Scott Brady (Gerald Tierney), Charles McGraw, Chuck (Kevin) Connors, and Mickey Shaughnessy won a deserved reputation as tough guys. Ed Begley, Arthur O'Connell, Kevin McCarthy, Dan O'Herlihy, and Richard Kiley established themselves as first-rate character actors. Among aspiring actresses, there were a number of promising ingenues who never quite made it to stardom, including Kathleen and Pat Crowley, Maggie McNamara, and Mary Murphy. Dorothy Malone (Maloney) did become a leading lady after winning an Oscar for a supporting role in 1957. Mercedes McCambridge, born of Irish parents on St. Patrick's Day, won plaudits for her portrayals of intense, neurotic women in character roles, but her screen appearances were intermittent, and she never played leads. Only Grace Kelly and Gene Kelly made it to the top and stayed there.

Several scenarists deserve mention for their work in the postwar period. Playwright Emmet Lavery began writing scripts for war films and won an Oscar nomination for his work on *The Court Martial of Billy Mitchell* (1955). But he probably obtained the most satisfaction in adapting for the screen his most successful plays, *The Magnificent Yankee* (1950) and *The First Legion* (1951), the former a sketch of Supreme Court Justice Oliver Wendell Holmes, the latter an insightful story of Jesuit priests. Frank S. Nugent, the half-Irish, half-Jewish film critic of the *New York Times* was hired by Darryl F. Zanuck after a glowing review of *The Grapes of Wrath* in 1940. Nugent's assignment was script-doctoring, improving screen plays so they would fare better with critics than the many Fox movies Nugent himself had panned in the *Times*. After World War II, Nugent became John Ford's principal scriptwriter, doing the screenplays for *The Quiet Man* and *The Last Hurrah* as well as a number of Ford Westerns. John Michael Hayes wrote scripts for Alfred Hitchcock from 1954 through 1956, and Richard Murphy made a specialty of scripting quasi-documentary features, such as Elia Kazan's *Boomerang* (1947) and *Panic in the Streets* (1950). Richard Breen proved very successful both alone and as a collaborator, winning an Oscar for his work on the screenplay of *Titanic* (1953). Don McGuire wrote a number of scripts in the 1950s; he also acted in and directed movies, wrote novels, and went on to a successful career in television.

Obviously, success stories were not lacking in the postwar years. But it was harder to make it in Hollywood in the 1950s. As the major studios cut back production, there were fewer opportunities for neophytes to learn their craft and receive proper guidance in planning their careers. The Hollywood of the Moguls, rapidly passing from the scene in this period, had its shortcomings, but it also had real advantages for talented newcomers.

☆ ☆ ☆ **6**

Lost and Found, 1960–

When President John F. Kennedy visited Ireland in 1963, an Irishman remarked to an American in Dublin: "It was nice of him to come, you know. It means a lot to our people, but you can't get around the impression that he is much more of you than he is of us."[1] This observation was astute but not surprising. Kennedy was much more American than Irish; he was also "a dramatic symbol of the distance traveled by the Irish in the United States."[2] The first "Irish Brahmin" not only helped to alter the stereotype of the Irish politician; his election to the presidency in 1960 and the universal mourning that followed his assassination in Dallas three years later was compelling proof of Irish Catholic acceptance in their adopted land. John F. Kennedy was the great-grandson of a famine immigrant, one of the 80 percent of Irish Catholics who are today third- or fourth-generation Irish Americans. Although Kennedy obviously outdistanced others in this group, the evidence available shows that Irish Catholics have done very well in the years since his election.

In education, income, and occupation, Irish Catholics are well above the national average for whites. In fact, having reached parity with British Protestants in these areas, they are the most successful ethnic group in America apart from the Jewish population. They are almost twice as likely to graduate from college as the general population, and the influx of Irish Catholics on college and university faculties since 1960 indicates that their representation in the profession of higher education will soon exceed their percentage of the general population. This development should make good the lack of an intellectual tradition that handicapped the Irish (and other Catholic ethnic groups).

High fertility has declined among Irish Americans (as well as permanent celibacy), making their families the same size as those of other Americans. Although alcoholism is still a problem, it is no worse for Irish Americans than for English-American urban Protestants and some other ethnic groups. Politically and socially, the Irish seem to be the most liberal non-Jewish group in the nation: the most likely to support racial integration, civil liberties, and feminism, and the most sexually tolerant. Only 17 percent disapprove of birth control; 28 percent, divorce; and 50 percent, premarital sex. Their attitude toward abortion is much the same as that of the general population.

Although more than 50 percent of the bishops and 34 percent of the priests in the American Catholic church were Irish in 1970, that church changed considerably after 1960 and so did the Irish laity's attitude toward it. As with other ethnic groups (although to a lesser extent), there has been a decline in Irish Catholic religious observance in recent years, and the laity's permissive attitude on such questions as birth control and abortion put it at odds with Rome on these issues. Parochial schools are in decline partly because they are no longer relevant to the concerns of many Catholics. With the development of its own intellectual leaders, the Irish laity no longer looks for direction to the clergy as it once did. The laity remains loyal to the church, but its members are no longer blindly obedient to clerical authority, and they are more individualistic in the practice of their religion. Their acceptance of the church is much more on their own terms than those of the Vatican. Once condemned by Rome, "Americanism" in the church seems to have triumphed—among most of the clergy as well as the laity. All this, coupled with the fact that American Protestants are now less fearful of papal influence and alien ideas, has brought the Irish into the mainstream of a culture that is now more tolerant and secular than ever before. Anti-Catholicism and anti-Irishness still exist, but they are much less potent than they were half a century or so ago.

In recent years ethnicity among the Irish, as among other minority groups, has undergone something of a revival, a development reflected in the boom in both American tourism in Ireland and Irish studies in this country. Many younger Irish Americans seem much more interested in their ethnic roots and heritage than were their parents. However, this quest for identity poses no threat to their place in the American cultural mainstream, partly because their forebears broadened that mainstream as they entered it. Any cultural changes resulting from the search for Irish roots are likely to be minor. Despite their interest in things Irish, American Hibernophiles have not embraced the ultraconservative values of Irish Catholicism, nor do they seem much concerned about the long-running troubles in Northern Ireland.[3]

Although not so successful as the Irish in the years since 1960, the movie industry made a modest comeback—coming to terms with television, winning back foreign markets through financing motion pictures made abroad, and becoming part of conglomerate enterprises, which supplied movie companies with capital and diversified their operations. By the midseventies, weekly attendance had been stabilized at around 20 million people in just under 15,000 theaters. Although the cost of making a theatrical movie rose steeply, to over $17 million by 1986, admission prices also rose, and blockbusters like *Jaws, Star Wars,* and *E.T.* reaped astronomic profits of more than $100 million each. As always, money decisions dominate the industry, and it remains oligopolistic, despite the federal government's seemingly successful trust-busting action in the 1940s.[4]

With television having long since replaced movies as the most influential mass medium, movie censorship is no longer a live issue. When the major companies lost control of their theaters and the Supreme Court extended to motion pictures full freedom of expression, both the PCA and the Legion of Decency began to lose power over film content. As early as 1953, producer Otto Preminger defied the PCA and released his mildly risque comedy *The Moon is Blue* without the PCA's seal of approval. Preminger's action and the movie's box office success were a setback for the censors and a sign of things to come. Sensing the change, Joe Breen resigned in 1954, after twenty years as head of the PCA. Minor revisions were made in the Production Code in the 1950s and a sweeping revision in 1966. In 1968 producers, distributors, and exhibitors supported the introduction of a new classification system, which reflected more permissive social attitudes toward such subjects as sex and street language. The new system, operated by a Code and Rating Administration (which replaced the PCA) undoubtedly succeeded in its aim of encouraging artistic freedom by expanding the limits of creativity, yet it also led to excesses by those who abused the new freedom. Following the example of the movie industry's regulatory agency, the National Catholic Office for Motion Pictures (as the Legion of Decency has been known since 1966) instituted more liberal guidelines for rating movies, but its power is only a shadow of that once wielded by the Legion of Decency.[5]

However "respectable" and successful in other fields in the two decades following John F. Kennedy's election to the presidency, the Irish continued to seek careers in show business, and a number of talented performers made their mark during this period. Some were bright and durable stars such as Steve McQueen, Ryan O'Neal, Ellen Burstyn (Edna Rae Gillooly), and Irish-born Peter O'Toole and Richard Harris. Others flourished more briefly, such as Ali (Alice) McGraw, Jennifer O'Neill, and Tatum O'Neal, Ryan's daughter. And some superb character actors and actresses emerged in the 1960s and 1970s, among them Jane Alexander (Quigley), Charles Durning, George Kennedy, Jackie Gleason, Art Carney, Eileen Brennan, Annette O'Toole, Peter Boyle, Patrick McGoohan, Carroll O'Connor, Milo O'Shea, Patrick O'Neal, Paul Dooley, Brian Dennehy, M. Emmet Walsh, Mickey Rourke, and Michael Moriarty. In keeping with the changing times, few of these performers played "Irish" roles. And directors like Robert Mulligan and Burt Kennedy did not direct "Irish" films. Frank Gilroy, whose father was an Irish immigrant, wrote for television, stage, and screen, adapting his work for the movies and eventually directing them as well.

Although the relaxation of restrictions on film content was not an unmixed blessing, it did result in the production of some notable films with Irish subjects. One of these, *Ryan's Daughter* (1970), was actually a British production, but Robert Mitchum headed its cast, and it was filmed in lavish Hollywood style on the west coast of Ireland. Directed by the brilliant David Lean, whose credits include *The Bridge on the River Kwai* and *Lawrence of Arabia, Ryan's Daughter* is a romantic melodrama set against the background of World War I and the 1916 Easter Rising. The film boasts marvelous cinematography (which won an Oscar), generally good performances, and a degree of realism in its depiction of the mores and manners of Irish village life. But it is too long (176 minutes) and not well paced, and the magnificent scenery dominates both the players and the commonplace story, in which the crime of informing again plays an important part. In short, the movie does not measure up to Lean's other historical spectacles.

Irish family life was stripped of its sentimental facade in the screen versions of two powerful plays, Frank Gilroy's *The Subject Was Roses* (1968) and Eugene O'Neill's *Long Day's Journey into Night* (1962), neither of which had an Irish director or featured Irish players (with the exception of Martin Sheen, who played Timmy in *Roses* and whose mother was Irish). *The Subject Was Roses* is set in the Bronx at the close of World War II, when the return of John and Nettie Cleary's soldier-son Timmy triggers a confrontation between an angry, frustrated husband and a long-suffering, embittered wife. John Cleary is a drinker and a womanizer, who, according to the resentful Nettie, is "at his best in an impersonal situation." Both parents are jealous in their love of Timmy, yet find it hard to express that love to him. In the end, Timmy leaves home to make a life of his own, with his parents sadly but realistically supporting his decision.

The five characters in O'Neill's autobiographical masterwork are "distinctive individuals and also archetypes of American Irish character."[6] James Tyrone, the father, is a successful actor whose life has been scarred by his childhood poverty. His wife Mary is "lace-curtain Irish," a pathetic figure whom James's miserliness has turned into a drug addict. The older son, Jamie, is a drunken, self-destructive wastrel, and the younger son, Edmund (O'Neill himself), is the introspective, brooding "black Irishman." The maid, Cathleen, is an ignorant greenhorn, "just off the boat." In this story of one day in the life of the Tyrones in the summer of 1912, Edmund discovers that he has a mild case of tuberculosis and must go to a sanatorium, while his mother, recently released from a different kind of sanatorium, relapses into her morphine addiction. O'Neill tells his story "in terms of the deepest human emotions—love, hate, pride, envy, remorse. He has also told the story of the Irish Catholics in America in terms of his personal understanding of their long journey."[7] The motion picture does full justice to the play and its author.

A much more sensational treatment of the tensions of Irish family life and contemporary society was *Looking for Mr. Goodbar* (1977), starring Diane Keaton as Theresa Dunn and Richard Kiley as her sexually puritanical and insensitive father. *Goodbar* is a story of guilt, sexual repression and promiscuity, misogyny, and violence. By day a dedicated teacher of handicapped children in New York City, Theresa Dunn by night is a frequenter of singles' bars who engages in sexual encounters with male pickups. Unable to win her father's love and frustrated by the constraints of her religion, Theresa seeks emotional release through promiscuity. Her problems are resolved and her agony ended when she is brutally murdered by a drifter whom she has taken to her bed. The film was based on an actual murder case, and although director Richard Brooks does exploit the sexual aspects of the subject, he offers a sometimes graphic portrayal of the stress and neurosis that seem an integral part of life in today's society.[8]

Another kind of film entirely is *The Molly Maguires* (1970), directed by Martin Ritt, written by Walter Bernstein, and filmed on location around Wilkes-Barre, Pennsylvania. The story takes place in the anthracite coal fields in 1876, at a time when Irish Catholic miners were locked in a deadly struggle with rapacious WASP and Irish Protestant mineowners. Although the film does take serious historical liberties, portraying the Mollies as frustrated but well-intentioned advocates of labor's rights and playing down their vicious terrorism,[9] it nevertheless offers a graphic and honest picture of life in the mines and company towns—the miners' back-breaking and dangerous toil, their squalid living conditions, the brutality of the company police, the parish priest's futile denunciations of violence, the inhumanity of a system that prevailed in the nation's coalfields well into the twentieth century.

The story traces the developing relationship between the Mollies' leader, Jack Kehoe (Sean Connery), and James McParlan (Richard Harris), the Pinkerton detective whose mission is to infiltrate and destroy the secret society. Although bitter experience has taught McParlan what he must do to get ahead in his adopted country, he becomes increasingly ambivalent about his assignment (unlike the real McParlan who detested the Mollies). Warming to Kehoe, McParlan tries to get him to abandon violence before it destroys him and the miners' cause. Infected by Kehoe's rage, he even joins in a frenzied destruction of that symbol of oppression, the company store. In the end, however, McParlan's ambition wins out, and his testimony sends Kehoe and other Mollies to the gallows. But the film's final scenes show clearly how much McParlan's obsession "to look down, not up" has cost him. He is the worst of all Irish pariahs, the informer who has betrayed his own people. The movie says volumes about the Irish struggle to make a better life in America in the face of many of the same heartbreaking obstacles they faced in Ireland.

The Molly Maguires also says something about the continuing bitterness over Hollywood's moral cowardice during the Red scare. Ritt and Bernstein, having refused to "name names" for HUAC, were both blacklisted during the 1950s and expressed their detestation of informers and informing in *The Molly Maguires* (and *The Front* [1976]). Like Kazan and Schulberg in *On the Waterfront*, Ritt and Bernstein deliberately used Irish characters to make their point. To Ritt, Sean Connery is the hero of the film, and Harris's sympathetic portrayal of McParlan is presumably intended to make his final betrayal of his comrades all the worse. The movie cost an impressive $9 million but did very poorly at the box office. Ritt attributes the commercial failure to the film's being too complicated for its audience, with the leading character painted gray rather than black or white.[10] In fact, the failure was probably due largely to the ignorance of prospective patrons about the Molly Maguires and an ill-conceived advertising campaign that did nothing to enlighten them.

The Miracle Worker (1962) offers a view of the Irish-American experience that is as grim as that of *The Molly Maguires* but one that is also much more positive. Based on William Gibson's prize-winning play of the same name, *The Miracle Worker* depicts the childhood of Helen Keller, the blind and deaf Alabama girl whose later achievements made her world famous. In a searing, unforgettable performance that won her an Oscar for best actress, Anne Bancroft (Italiano) portrays Helen's teacher, the half-blind Annie Sullivan from Boston.[11] Annie's anguished recollections—in dreams and conscious memories—reveal the poverty and suffering that traumatized her early years. Raised as an orphan with her tubercular brother in a state alms house, the blind Annie is determined somehow to have her sight restored, to go to school, and never to "give up." It is this unquenchable spirit that saves her life (though it cannot save her brother's), helps obtain the operations that partially restore her sight, makes her the class valedictorian at a leading school for the blind, and achieves the miraculous breakthrough that makes possible the education of Helen Keller, whose lifelong companion Annie becomes. The interaction between Annie and Helen is the subject of the film, the wrenching scenes they share, its highlights; but Annie's struggle to make Helen "see" is made much more understandable and moving by what we learn of Annie's own childhood. And that childhood, with its deprivation and perseverance, is an apt reminder of the experience of the pioneers of the urban ghetto.

Two other examples of realistic and dramatically effective films about the Irish are *The Friends of Eddie Coyle* (1973) and *True Confessions* (1981), both adapted from novels by Irish-American writers. *Eddie Coyle* is the seamy story of a small-time crook (beautifully played by the underrated actor, Robert Mitchum) trapped in a labyrinth of crime and corruption. Authentic settings, dialogue, and accents reflect author George V. Higgins' mastery of the Boston Irish subculture. *True Confessions* is also a story of crime and corruption, equally evocative of time and place (Los Angeles in the late 1940s), but is a more subtle and ambitious film. Monsignor Desmond Spellacy (Robert de Niro) is a new kind of movie priest, one spiritually tormented by his success as an ecclesiastical careerist. His brother Tom (Robert Duvall), a homicide detective, is tormented, too—disgusted with himself and the corruption and hypocrisy that surround him, and ambivalent toward Des. Enraged at the honor bestowed by the church on a prominent Catholic layman (Charles Durning) and by his brother's association with him, Tom becomes obsessed with exposing the man's sordid past, even though such exposure will serve no practical end and will wreck Des's career. In the end, half-regretfully, half-gratefully, Des humbly accepts the moral demands made by his brother and his own conscience, losing the world to save his own soul. Although not as richly textured and satirical as John Gregory

Dunne's novel, *True Confessions* is a memorable film, despite or perhaps because of the fact that its director and most of its cast were not Irish.

A more recent specimen of Irish film noir is *Ironweed* (1987), an adaptation of William Kennedy's Pulitzer Prize-winning novel, starring Jack Nicholson. Very early in his screen career, Nicholson, who is Irish on his father's side, played Weary Reilly in the unsuccessful film version of James T. Farrell's *Studs Lonigan* (1960). In 1976 he won a richly deserved Academy Award for his performance as the exuberant but doomed nonconformist Randel Patrick McMurphy in *One Flew Over the Cuckoo's Nest* (1975), and in *Reds* (1981) he was first rate as the youthful, cynical Eugene O'Neill. In *Ironweed* Nicholson eschews his usual insolent charm in his portrayal of Francis Phelan, a haunted, guilt-ridden derelict who wanders the streets of his hometown of Albany, New York, in the autumn of 1938. Although he is an Irish Catholic, Phelan's strengths and weaknesses transcend ethnicity, making him part of the universal human condition. Nicholson's incisive performance illumines the character and sustains the somber mood of William Kennedy's screenplay.

Contemporary Boston is the setting for *The Verdict* (1982), the story of a down-and-out lawyer named Frank Galvin (Paul Newman) who finds personal and professional salvation in a medical malpractice case. The story is compelling and the acting first rate, but what Irish flavor there is in *The Verdict* comes largely from the characters' names, rather than from the plot, dialogue, or the characters themselves. This is even more true of Newman's two 1981 movies, *Fort Apache, The Bronx* and *Absence of Malice,* in which the names of the characters he plays—Murphy and Gallagher—are the only things Irish about the films.

John Huston's *The Dead* (1987) provides a fitting conclusion to this discussion of Irish films. An adaptation of James Joyce's famous short story, *The Dead* was the last film Huston directed, completed only shortly before his death. Although he was not of Irish stock, Huston made his home in Ireland for two decades after 1953, becoming an Irish citizen in 1964. He sometimes used Irish locations for his movies, but he never made one about the Irish until *The Dead,* a story he had long wanted to film. Although ill health compelled Huston to make the movie in California rather than Ireland, the cast was all Irish, except for his daughter Anjelica, but even she was raised in Ireland. Huston's intimate knowledge of filmmaking, of literary adaptation, and of Irish life and culture is abundantly evident in *The Dead*. In this culmination of a long and distinguished career, Huston's mature artistic vision illuminates the youthful Joyce's epiphany of the mortality of life and love. The director's son Tony, who wrote the screenplay, as well as daughter Anjelica and the marvelous Irish players share credit for this brilliant cinematic achievement.

Hollywood's forays into realism during the last three decades did not mean that moviemakers had lost their taste or touch for fantasy, satire, and stereotypes. John Wayne's *McQ* (1974) and *Brannigan* (1976), and Clint Eastwood's "Dirty Harry" Callahan raised the Irish cop to new heights of celebrity by lowering him to new depths of violence. Similar to these characters was "Popeye" Doyle, the screen counterpart of a real-life NYPD detective whose exploits were dramatized in *The French Connection* (1971), a film which won five Academy Awards, including those for best picture and best actor (Gene Hackman). Roy Scheider's Francis McNeill Murphy, a burned-out Vietnam veteran and police helicopter pilot, took the Irish cop off the street and lifted him into the sky with the latest technology of surveillance and destruction in *Blue Thunder* (1983). *Outland* (1981) went even further, sending Sean Connery's U.S. Marshal W. T. O'Neil to the Third Moon of Jupiter in an outer space version of *High Noon*. Connery returned to earth with a bang in his Oscar-winning performance as Officer Jimmy Malone, an honest Chicago cop who becomes a federal agent battling Al Capone in *The Untouchables* (1987). In *The Godfather* (1972), Sterling Hayden gave a striking portrayal of a corrupt New York police captain, and Geraldine Page was even more impressive as the formidable mother of a corrupt cop in *The Pope of Greenwich Village* (1984). Robert Shaw was full of menace as the Depression era gangster Doyle Lonnegan in *The Sting* (1973), whereas his fellow Englishman Bob Hoskins played a less violent but real-life mobster, the well-known Owney Madden, in *The Cotton Club* (1984). In that wonderful spoof of the Warner Bros., productions of the 1930s, *Movie, Movie* (1978), George C. Scott was "Gloves" Malloy, the crusty, honest fight manager; Trish van Devere was Betsy McGuire, the virginal librarian; and Ann

Reinking was "Troubles" Moran, the distinctly nonvirginal chanteuse, a parody done even better by Lesley Ann Warren as Norma Cassidy in *Victor/Victoria* (1982). Michael Keaton played Johnny Kelly who became gangster *Johnny Dangerously* (1984), a mediocre take-off of Cagney gangster movies. In the riotous film version of screenwriter Ben Hecht's early memoirs, *Gaily, Gaily* (1969), Brian Keith played Francis Sullivan, a hard-drinking Chicago newspaperman whose forte was sensationalism, and Hume Cronyn was "Honest Tim" Grogan, political boss and boodler, c. 1910. Robert Duvall continued the Irish military tradition, appearing as Lieutenant Colonel "Bull' Meechum, a "gung ho" Marine fighter pilot in *The Great Santini* (1979). Playing a real-life warrior, Cliff Robertson portrayed Lieutenant (j.g.) John F. Kennedy in *PT-109* (1963), an account of JFK's World War II adventures in the South Pacific. Musicals were becoming too expensive to film by the 1970s, but Debbie Reynolds gave a rousing performance as a previously unsung Irish-American heroine in *The Unsinkable Molly Brown* (1964). *Finian's Rainbow* (1968), on the other hand, sank like a stone, a badly filmed version of an outdated musical fantasy play of the late 1940s. Not much more successful was the attempt to update the Irish priest persona in the screen adaptation of the successful play *Mass Appeal* (1985), which featured Jack Lemmon as Father Tim Farley and Charles Durning as Monsignor Tom Burke.

The fact that the Irish are not often portrayed realistically in films is nothing new. What is novel and disturbing is the resort to starkly negative stereotypes in movies that purport to be realistic. In *Joe* (1970), Joe Curran (Peter Boyle) is a caricatured bigot that puts the Ku Klux Klan to shame. A foul-mouthed hard hat who spouts racist and chauvinistic nonsense, Joe hates blacks, hippies, liberals, commies, and, in fact, just about everybody. A "real American" who feels threatened by alien ideas and people different from himself, Joe thinks he has become an outsider in his own country. He hates blacks because he believes that they are coddled by the government and the media; he hates hippies (and not so secretly envies their sexual license) because they have enjoyed advantages that they never earned and he never had. In the end, he and a WASP ally, Bill Compton (Dennis Patrick), run amuck in a bloody, mindless massacre at a hippie commune. The movie is unfair to hard hats, lower middle-class Americans, and people named Joe Curran. It is also unfair to one of the most liberal ethnic groups—the Irish. The movie is a cartoon, but it is not at all funny. Nor does it make any useful contribution to understanding the trauma suffered by the United States in the late 1960s and early 1970s.[12]

Ragtime (1981) is an even more striking example of negative Irish stereotyping. The film's setting is New York City during the first decade of this century. James Cagney, emerging from a twenty-year retirement, plays Police Commissioner Rhinelander Waldo, a pillar of the establishment who cold-bloodedly orders the killing of the movie's black antihero, Coalhouse Walker (Howard Rollins). And if this reversal of roles for Cagney is not enough of a departure from Hollywood tradition, the depiction of the Irishmen who torment Walker as racist troglodytes certainly is. The characterization of Willie Conklin (Kenneth Macmillan), the captain of the Emerald Isle Volunteer Fire Company, is not far removed from the vicious nativist caricatures of the Irish a century ago. Had Coalhouse Walker or Tateh (Mandy Patinkin), the movie's principal Jewish character, been as savagely depicted as Willie Conklin, *Ragtime* would surely have aroused a storm of protest for its white racism or anti-Semitism. The Irish, however, have again become fair game for some social critics. Once they were pilloried by the WASP elite. Now the success that has made them part of the American establishment has also made them safe and inviting targets for enemies of that establishment.[13]

The Irish in *Ragtime* are reviled less for what they were at the turn of the century than for what they would become as they scaled the social ladder. America no longer fears the Irish as subversive aliens, nor does it patronize and applaud them as upward-bound underdogs. But it sometimes resents them for making good, and this resentment hinders balanced portrayals. Like virtually all white Americans in the Ragtime era, the Irish were racist, but to define them solely by that characteristic is no more accurate than the stereotypical definitions offered by *The Public Enemy, Going My Way,* or *The Quiet Man.* And it is more harmful.

In the light of recent developments, one can understand why Irish Americans have become almost a "lost statistical category."[14] And why an Irish-American scholar can lament: "Irish identity is going, going, and soon it will be gone. And it will be difficult—probably impossible—for the American Irish to recover something that has almost disappeared."[15]

The title of this chapter is derived from the fact that the Irish have indeed lost most of their ethnic distinctiveness in today's America,[16] but that a good deal of what has been lost can be found in the movies. Despite their factual distortions, movies since the days of Edison reveal a lot about how America perceived the Irish, how that perception gradually changed, and what role moviemakers had in changing it. During the "silent era," the "stage Irish" stereotypes were softened, making them less offensive and more attractive. And during the quarter-century following the introduction of sound, the more mellow traditional stereotypes were joined by new dramatis personae—the Irish priest, the Irish antihero, and the Irish All-American, all of whom quickly became part of our popular culture. This growing popularity on the screen mirrored and assisted Irish social progress. At the same time, the prominent role played by Irish Catholics in the Legion of Decency and the Production Code Administration increased their influence in Hollywood and further enhanced the Irish screen image, helping to complete Irish assimilation.

From the nickelodeon's "stage Irishman" to the presidency of a former movie actor named Reagan is a long road, leading from "Pat and Bridget" to All-American types such as Michael J. Fox, Matthew Broderick, Matt Dillon, Kelly McGillis, Elizabeth McGovern, and Meg Ryan. To travel that road is to discover not only how America changed the Irish, but also how the Irish changed America. The Irish built the Catholic church in this country and made it an integral part of American society. They played a vital role in such fields as politics, law enforcement, the labor movement, the armed services, journalism, and sports. They enriched our language and literature, our music and dance. They even made the feast day of Ireland's patron saint an American national celebration. And all this was reflected in the movies, in which the Irish also played a leading role—Ford, Cagney, Tracy, O'Brien, Grace Kelly, and Gene Kelly, and all the others who came before and after them. In becoming American off screen and on, the Irish changed America and themselves, in both cases for the better.

Notes

INTRODUCTION

1. Patrick J. Blessing, "The Irish," *Harvard Encyclopedia of American Ethnic Groups*, ed. Stephen Thernstrom (Cambridge, Mass.: The Belknap Press, 1980), 524.

2. Garth Jowett, *Film: The Democratic Art* (Boston: Little, Brown, 1976), 457.

3. Charles Fanning, "Mr. Dooley in Chicago: Finley Peter Dunne as Historian of the Irish in America," *America and Ireland, 1776–1976: The American Identity and the Irish Connection,* eds. David Noel Doyle and Owen Dudley Edwards (Westport, Conn.: Greenwood Press, 1980), 163.

CHAPTER 1

1. U.S. Bureau of the Census, *Statistical Abstract of the United States: 1985* (105th ed.), Washington, D.C., 1984, 35; Andrew M. Greeley, *The Irish Americans: The Rise to Money and Power* (New York: Harper and Row, 1981), 6. Since there is no federal religious census and the 40 million Irish include many of mixed ancestry, only a rough estimate of the number of Irish Catholics in the United States is possible.

2. Kerby A. Miller, *Emigrants and Exiles: Ireland and the Irish Exodus to North America* (New York: Oxford University Press, 1985), 137, 169, 193.

3. The results of this assimilation process are demonstrated in such movies as *The Cheyenne Social Club* (1970) and *Murphy's Romance* (1985). In the former, the fact the two cowboy protagonists (James Stewart and Henry Fonda) are named John O'Hanlon and Harley Sullivan has no ethnic or religious significance whatsoever. The same is true of the characters Murphy Jones (James Garner) and Emma Moriarty (Sally Ann Field) in the latter, a film set in contemporary Arizona.

4. Marjorie R. Fallows, *Irish Americans: Identity and Assimilation* (Englewood Cliffs, N.J.: Prentice-Hall, 1979), 2. On the Scotch-Irish, see Fallows, 6, 20–22, 64–65; Miller, *Emigrants*, 131–279; Joe R. Feagin, *Racial and Ethnic Relations* (Englewood Cliffs, N.J.: Prentice-Hall, 1978), 82–85; Thomas Sowell, *Ethnic America: A History* (New York: Basic Books, 1981), 22–24; Maldwyn A. Jones, "The Scotch-Irish," *Harvard Encyclopedia of American Ethnic Groups*, 895–908.

5. Miller, *Emigrants*, 291, 346; Patrick J. Blessing, "The Irish," *Harvard Encyclopedia of American Ethnic Groups*, ed. Stephen Thernstrom (Cambridge: The Belknap Press, 1980), 528.

6. Philip Gleason, "American Identity and Americanization," *Harvard Encyclopedia of American Ethnic Groups*, 34–35; Thomas Archdeacon, *Becoming American: An Ethnic History* (New York: The Free Press, 1983), 74.

7. L. P. Curtis, Jr., *Anglo-Saxons and Celts: A Study of Anti-Irish Prejudice in Victorian England* (Bridgeport, Conn.: Conference on British Studies, 1968), 53.

8. George Potter, *To the Golden Door: The Story of the Irish in Ireland and America* (Boston: Little, Brown, 1960), 156; Pat O'Brien, *The Wind at My Back: The Life and Times of Pat O'Brien* (New York: Doubleday, 1964), 30–31; Maureen Murphy, "Irish-American Theatre," *Ethnic Theatre in the United States*, ed. Maxine Schwartz Seller (Westport, Conn.: Greenwood Press, 1983), 222; On nativism and Irish stereotypes, see also: Potter, *To the Golden Door*, 164, 167; O'Brien, *Wind*, 32–33; Archdeacon, *Becoming*, 74–75; Curtis, *Anglo-Saxons*, 90–97; Miller, *Emigrants*, 275–279; Gleason, "American Identity," 34–37; Blessing, "The Irish," 527–533; Thomas T. McAvoy, C.S.C., *A History of the Catholic Church in the United States* (Notre Dame, Ind.: University of Notre Dame Press, 1969), 137–145; Lawrence J. McCaffrey, *The Irish Diaspora in America* (Bloomington: Indiana University Press, 1976), 85–106; Greeley, *Irish Americans*, 76–78.

9. Blessing, "The Irish," 530.

10. Greeley, *Irish Americans*, 76; on this subject, see also 74–76. Also on this subject, see Blessing, "The Irish," 531–532; Miller, *Emigrants*, 313–321; Sowell, *Ethnic America*, 17–18, 28–29; Carl Wittke, *The Irish*

in America (Baton Rouge: Louisiana State University Press, 1956), 32–51, 62–74.

11. Richard Stivers, *A Hair of the Dog: Irish Drinking and American Stereotype* (University Park: Pennsylvania State University Press, 1976), *passim*, but especially, 64–67, 86–90, 128–131, 139–180; William B. Helmreich, *The Things They Say Behind Your Back* (New York: Doubleday, 1982), 142–147, 152–156; Greeley, *Irish Americans*, 62, 115–120, 171–182; Miller, *Emigrants*. 319–320; Potter, *Golden Door*, 517–520; McCaffrey, *Irish Diaspora*, 78–79; Archdeacon, *Becoming*, 72–73.

12. Greeley, *Irish Americans*, 121–129.

13. McAvoy, *History*, 2–3, 148, 270–272; Archdeacon, *Becoming*, 111; James Hennesey, *American Catholics: A History of the Roman Catholic Community in the United States* (New York: Oxford University Press, 1981), 126, 194; John Higham, *Strangers in the Land: Patterns of American Nativism, 1860–1925* (New York: Atheneum, 1969), 75; Robert D. Cross, "The Irish," *Ethnic Leadership in America*, ed. John Higham (Baltimore: Johns Hopkins University Press, 1978), 181–184.

14. Cross, "Irish," 178–181; Archdeacon, *Becoming*, 79–80; Feagin, *Racial and Ethnic America*, 90–91; Sowell, *Ethnic America*, 35, 39–41; Thomas N. Brown, "The Political Irish: Politicians and Rebels," *America and Ireland, 1776–1976*, 137–139.

15. Wittke, *Irish*, 135–149.

16. Thomas N. Brown, *Irish-American Nationalism, 1870–1890* (Philadelphia: J. B. Lippincott, 1966), 23–24, 31, 41; McCaffrey, *Irish Diaspora*, 110–111; William V. Shannon, *The American Irish* (New York: Macmillan, 1963), 132–135.

17. McCaffrey, *Irish Diaspora*, 72–73; Emmet Larkin, "The Devotional Revolution in Ireland," *The Historical Dimensions of Irish Catholicism* (Washington, D.C.: Catholic University of America Press, 1984), 5–10, 57–89.

18. Miller, *Emigrants*, 499–500.

19. On the American Irish, c. 1865–1915, see McCaffrey, *Irish Diaspora*, 79–82; Miller, *Emigrants*, 495–506; Blessing, "The Irish," 531–538; Cross, "The Irish," 186–191; Higham, *Strangers*, 26, 60–67, 86–87.

20. Potter, *Golden Door*, 609.

21. Murphy, "Irish American," 226.

22. Samuel G. Freedman, "What Musicals and Comedy Owe to Harrigan and Hart," *New York Times*, January 27, 1985, Section 2, p. 4.

23. Murphy, "Irish American," 226–227; Freedman, "Musicals," 1 and 4; E. J. Kahn, Jr., *The Merry Partners: The Age and Stage of Harrigan and Hart* (New York: Random House, 1955), *passim*.

24. Murphy, "Irish American," 227–229; Wittke, *Irish,* 253–263; Shannon, *American Irish,* 142–143; Stivers, *Hair,* 155–159; Blessing, "The Irish," 539; Albert F. McLean, Jr., *American Vaudeville as Ritual* (Lexington: University of Kentucky Press, 1965), 23, 121; Kathleen Donovan, "Good Old Pat: An Irish American Stereotype in Decline," *Eire-Ireland* 15.3 (1980), 6–14.

25. It is worth mentioning here that very few of the Irish who entered the world of popular entertainment saw fit to change their names to something that sounded more "American," i.e., WASP. When such a change did take place, it was usually the result of an Irishwoman changing her name by marriage. For every Fred Allen and John Ford, there were legions of Cohans, Kellys, O'Briens, Ryans, and Moores. This was not the case with other ethnic minorities, such as the Jews and the Italians, who often had their names "Americanized." Indeed, some non-Irish performers even adopted Irish names to aid their careers. This sort of "depersonalization" is now largely a thing of the past. The Irish may have escaped it partly because of their stubborn ethnic pride, but their good fortune probably owes more to the fact that Irish names were already partly Anglicized when the Irish came to America and that these names were both more familiar and more easily pronounceable by people of British stock than German, Slavic, Latin, or Jewish names.

CHAPTER 2

1. Tino Balio, ed., *The American Film Industry* (Madison: University of Wisconsin Press, 1976), 3–18; Ephraim Katz, *The Film Encyclopedia* (New York: Perigee Books, 1979), 374.

2. Balio, *American Film,* 103–114; Katz, *Film,* 835–836, 893, 1265; Douglas Gomery, *The Hollywood Studio System* (London: Macmillan, 1986), 26–28.

3. Richard Maltby, *Harmless Entertainment: Hollywood and the Ideology of Consensus* (Metuchen, N.J.: Scarecrow Press, 1983), 95–96.

4. Garth Jowett, *Film: The Democratic Art* (Boston: Little, Brown, 1976), 108–109, 250; Arthur F. McClure, "Censor the Movies! Early Attempts to Regulate the Content of Motion Pictures in America, 1907–1936," *The Movies: An American Idiom—Readings in the Social History of the American Motion Picture,* ed. Arthur F. McClure (Rutherford, N.J.: Fairleigh Dickinson Press, 1971), 117–124.

5. Jowett, *Film,* 62.

6. Lewis Jacobs, *The Rise of the American Film: A Critical History* (New York: Columbia University, 1968, originally published in 1939), 19–20.

7. Kemp R. Niver, *Motion Pictures From the Library of Congress Paper Print Collection, 1894–1912* (Berkeley: University of California Press, 1967); Roger B. Dooley, "The Irish on the Screen: I," *Films in Review* 8.5 (1957), 212. The films mentioned in the text, except for *The Kansas Saloon Smashers,* may be viewed at the Motion Picture, Broadcasting and Recorded Sound Division of the Library of Congress, Washington, D.C.

8. John Higham, *Strangers in the Land: Patterns of American Nativism, 1860–1925* (New York: Atheneum, 1969), 122.

9. Ibid, 116–124.

10. Jacobs, *Rise,* 152–153.

11. Ibid., 123, 153; Katz, *Film,* 874–875; George Mitchell, "Sidney Olcott," *Films in Review* 5.4 (1954), 175–181.

12. The three films discussed, as well as Olcott's film about Emmet, are available for viewing in the Library of Congress. *Son of Erin* is unfortunately incomplete, and the three surviving reels are somewhat mixed up in sequence, but the main outlines of the plot are clear enough.

13. Jacobs, *Rise,* 88, 127. The information on film artists in my study is largely taken from Katz's indispensable *Film Encyclopedia.*

14. Terry Ramsaye, *A Million and One Nights: A History of the Motion Picture* (New York: Simon and Schuster, 1926), II, 468–472, 715.

15. Balio, *American Film,* 112–116; Jowett, *Film,* 475.

16. Lester D. Friedman, *Hollywood's Image of the Jew* (New York: Frederick Ungar, 1982), 60–61; Raymond Moley, *The Hays Office* (Indianapolis: Bobbs–Merrill, 1945), 22–23; Patricia Erens, *The Jew in American Cinema* (Bloomington: Indiana University Press, 1984), 53–54, 76–77.

17. Jowett, *Film,* 338.

18. Ibid., 172, 181–182.

19. Balio, *American Film,* 116–118.

20. Benjamin B. Hampton, *History of the American Film Industry from its Beginnings to 1931* (New York: Dover Publications, 1970), 80–81, 337; Gomery, *Hollywood,* 90; Katz, *Film,* 1049; *New York Times,* July 26, 1945, 19.

21. Gomery, *Hollywood,* 68; Billy Grady, *The Irish Peacock: The Confessions of a Legendary Talent Agent* (New Rochelle, N.Y.: Arlington House, 1972).

22. Richard J. Whalen, *The Founding Father: The Story of Joseph P. Kennedy* (New York: New American Library, 1964), 75–99; Balio, *American Film,* 118; Gomery, *Hollywood,* 124–126.

23. Katz, *Film,* 1039–1040; Frank Manchel, *Film Study: A Resource Guide* (Rutherford, N.J.: Fairleigh Dickinson Press, 1973), 175–176.

24. Katz, *Film*, 977–978.

25. Jacobs, *Rise*, 380–381.

26. John, Lionel, and Ethel Barrymore were not of Irish Catholic stock, although many people believed that they were. They were the offspring of an English actor, Herbert Blythe, and an American actess, Georgiana Drew, whose mother was English and whose father was an Irish Protestant. The elder Blythe had adopted Barrymore as his stage name, and his children followed suit. This name, coupled with their mother's conversion to Roman Catholicism, which caused them to be raised as Roman Catholics, led many to think of them as Irish. John's tragic addiction to alcohol doubtless fostered this misconception.

27. Jacobs, *Rise*, 280–281.

28. Marjorie R. Fallows, *Irish Americans: Identity and Assimilation* (Englewood Cliffs, N.J.: Prentice-Hall, 1979), 46; Andrew M. Greeley, *The Irish Americans: The Rise to Money and Power* (New York: Harper and Row, 1981), 112–113; Kerby A. Miller, *Emigrants and Exiles: Ireland and the Irish Exodus to North America* (New York: Oxford University Press, 1985), 554–555; Nathan Glazer and Daniel Patrick Moynihan, *Beyond the Melting Pot: The Negroes, Puerto Ricans, Jews, Italians, and Irish of New York City* (Cambridge, Mass.: MIT Press and Harvard University Press, 1963), 253.

29. Actually, Smith was only one-quarter Irish. Of his four grandparents, only one was Irish, the others being English, Italian, and German. But Smith was perceived as Irish by the Irish and almost everyone else.

30. Lary May, *Screening Out the Past: The Birth of Mass Culture and the Motion Picture Industry* (New York: Oxford University Press, 1980), 257.

31. Kenneth W. Munden, ed., *The American Film Institute Catalog of Motion Pictures Produced in the United States: Feature Films, 1921–30* (New York: Bowker, 1971), 1553–1554.

32. The abbreviation LC or MOMA after a film means that a print is available for viewing at the Library of Congress or the Museum of Modern Art. However, both *Denny from Ireland* and *Ireland a Nation* are missing the first of their four reels.

33. For Ford's Irish films, see Chapter 4.

34. George Amberg, ed., *New York Times Film Reviews, 1913–1968*, 6 vols. (New York: Arno press, 1971), 1:376–377.

35. *New York Times*, July–October, 1927; Thomas Cripps, "The Movie Jew as an Image of Assimilation," *Journal of Popular Film* 4 (1975), 197–198.

36. Friedman, *Hollywood's Image*, 33.

37. Mari Kathleen Fielder, "Fatal Attraction: Irish-Jewish Romance in Early Film and Drama," *Eire-Ireland* 20.3 (1985), 13.

CHAPTER 3

1. Garth Jowett, *Film: The Democratic Art* (Boston: Little, Brown, 1976), 475. The figure of 90 million was not reached again until 1946, and by then it represented a smaller percentage of the population.

2. Jowett, *Film*, 475; Tino Balio, ed., *The American Film Industry* (Madison: University of Wisconsin Press, 1976), 214–218.

3. Lewis Jacobs, *The Rise of the American Film: A Critical History* (New York: Columbia University, 1968), 409–410; Andrew Bergman, *We're in the Money: Depression America and Its Films* (New York: New York University Press, 1971), 3–17; Peter Roffman and Jim Purdy, *The Hollywood Social Problem Film: Madness, Despair, and Politics from the Depression to the Fifties* (Bloomington: Indiana University Press, 1981), 15–20.

4. Although the Jews' disappearance from movies had several causes, one contributory factor was the studio bosses' own attitude toward their ethnic origins. Seeking assimilation for themselves and the broadest possible appeal for their product, Jewish film Moguls took pride in their Americanism, often married Gentile wives, and avoided Jewish subjects on the screen. In response to this "de-Semitizing" of the movies, the not uncommon practice of Anglicizing their names became standard for Jewish performers. Lester D. Friedman, *Hollywood's Image of the Jew* (New York: Frederick Ungar, 1982), 57, 64; Patricia Erens, *The Jew in American Cinema* (Bloomington: Indiana University Press, 1984), 135–139; Richard Maltby, *Harmless Entertainment: Hollywood and the Ideology of Consensus* (Metuchen, N.J.: Scarecrow Press, 1983), 152.

5. Jack L. Warner, with Dean Jennings, *My First Hundred Years in Hollywood* (New York: Random House, 1965), 207–208, 215–216, 220–224, 285.

6. Like his political counterpart Al Smith, Cagney was not all Irish. His maternal grandfather was Norwegian. James Cagney, *Cagney by Cagney* (New York: Pocket Books, 1977), 13, 21.

7. Ibid., 214.

8. Henry Cohen, ed., *The Public Enemy* (Madison: University of Wisconsin Press, 1981). Testimony to the movie's impact is provided by a description of a film whose plot is obviously largely derived from *The Public Enemy* and Studs Lonigan's reaction to it in *Judgment Day* (1935),

the final volume in James T. Farrell's *Studs Lonigan* trilogy, a work of painstaking social realism about Chicago Irish Americans, c. 1916–1931.

9. In fact, he had already made several movies.

10. Kenneth Tynan, *Curtains* (New York: Atheneum, 1961), 358–359.

11. Stanley Kauffmann, ed., with Bruce Henstall, *American Film Criticism: From the Beginnings to Citizen Kane* (New York: Liveright, 1972), 252; see also 250–251.

12. Ibid., 263–264.

13. Robert Wilson, ed., *The Film Criticism of Otis Ferguson* (Philadelphia: Temple University Press, 1971), 198.

14. Ibid., 278–279.

15. Jacobs, *Rise*, 515.

16. Maltby, *Harmless Entertainment*, 109; Thomas Schatz, *Hollywood Genres: Formulas, Filmmaking, and the Studio System* (Austin: University of Texas, 1981), 84.

17. Pat O'Brien, *The Wind at My Back: The Life and Times of Pat O'Brien* (New York: Doubleday, 1964), 128.

18. The Irish priest, an important character in his own right, is discussed in the final section of this chapter.

19. Cagney was also deemed unsuitable for the Rockne role—and perhaps that of Father Flanagan as well—because of his liberal political sympathies, notably his gestures of support for the Spanish Republic in the civil war of 1936–1939. A fervent New Dealer, Cagney began to move right politically after FDR's death in 1945. He became extremely conservative in his later years, as did another of the Warner Bros. ardent liberals of the 1930s and 1940s—Ronald Reagan. On the problems arising from Cagney's persona and politics, see Cagney, *Cagney*, 69, 77–78, 83, 126; Warner, *First*, 227–228; Patrick McGilligan, *Cagney: The Actor as Auteur*, rev. ed. (San Diego: A. S. Barnes, 1982), xiii, 49–53, 60–65, 145–148, 202–203; Rudy Behlmer, *Inside Warner Brothers (1935–1951)* (New York: Viking Penguin, 1985), 63, 113–114; Hal Wallis and Charles Higham, *Starmaker: The Autobiography of Hal Wallis* (New York: Macmillan, 1980), 67; Doug Warren, with James Cagney, *James Cagney: The Authorized Biography* (New York: St. Martin's Press, 1983), 118–119, 154.

20. Warren, *James Cagney*, 141.

21. With the possible exceptions of his roles as Lew Marsh, the alcoholic newspaper editor in *Come Fill the Cup* (1951), and Jake MacIllaney, the charmingly dishonest labor leader in *Never Steal Anything Small* (1959), Cagney never again played an urban antihero. The gangsters he played in *White Heat* (1949) and *Kiss Tomorrow Goodbye* (1950)

were not ethnic antiheroes but psychopathic killers. Much the same can be said of the IRA leader he played in *Shake Hands with the Devil* (1959), a sexually repressed political fanatic for whom killing had become a way of life.

22. Ted Sennett, *Warner Brothers Presents* (New Rochelle, N.Y.: Arlington House, 1971), 67.

23. McGilligan, *Cagney,* 17, 28, 35; Les and Barbara Keyser, *Hollywood and the Catholic Church: The Image of Roman Catholicism in American Movies* (Chicago: Loyola University Press, 1984), 61; Robert S. McElvaine, *The Great Depression: America, 1929–41* (New York: Times Books, 1983), 210–211; Nick Roddick, *A New Deal in Entertainment: Warner Brothers in the 1930s* (London: British Film Institute, 1983), 104–106, 117–118.

24. Nathan Glazer and Daniel Patrick Moynihan, *Beyond the Melting Pot: The Negroes, Puerto Ricans, Jews, Italians, and Irish of New York City* (Cambridge, Mass.: MIT Press and Harvard University Press, 1963), 246–247.

25. *Los Angeles Times*, March 31, 1986.

26. The revised code was mainly a list of specific prohibitions with a statement of reasons (the Lord draft of 1930) attached.

27. Cited in Kenneth Macgowan, *Behind the Screen: The History and Techniques of the Motion Picture* (New York: Delacorte Press, 1965), 359. On the Production Code and the Legion of Decency, see Daniel A. Lord, S. J., *Played by Ear: The Autobiography of Daniel A. Lord, S. J.* (Chicago: Loyola University Press, 1956), 269–313; Raymond Moley, *The Hays Office* (Indianapolis: Bobbs-Merrill, 1945), 68–93, 239–249; Maltby, *Harmless Entertainment,* 99–105, 152, 168; Jowett, *Film,* 246–256; Balio, *American Film,* 220–222; Bergman, *We're in the Money,* 3–6; Keyser, *Hollywood,* 57–60; Wilson, *Film Criticism,* 403–405; Behlmer, *Inside,* 31–32, 66–67; Roddick, *New Deal,* 34–39; James Hennesey, *American Catholics: A History of the Roman Catholic Community in the United States* (New York: Oxford University Press, 1981), 265; Murray Schumach, *The Face on the Cutting Room Floor* (New York: William Morrow, 1964), 84–89; Jack Vizzard, *See No Evil: Life Inside a Hollywood Censor* (New York: Simon and Schuster, 1970), 44–51, 175–177, 296–297.

28. *New York Times*, October 16, 1983.

29. Unlike his longtime friend O'Brien, Tracy was only half-Irish. His mother, née Carrie Brown, was descended from an old New England family. Larry Swindell, *Spencer Tracy . . . A Biography* (New York: World, 1969), 2–3.

30. Ibid., *passim;* Garson Kanin, *Tracy and Hepburn: An Intimate Memoir* (New York: Viking Press, 1971), 182; Warren, *James Cagney,* 132.

31. Ephraim Katz, *The Film Encyclopedia* (New York: Perigee Books, 1979), 1145.

32. Kanin, *Tracy and Hepburn,* 50.

33. Swindell, *Spencer Tracy,* 129–131.

34. Wilson, *Film Criticism,* 235.

35. For a discussion of *The Last Hurrah,* see pp. 82–83.

36. Kanin, *Tracy and Hepburn,* 24–26; "The Spencer Tracy Legacy: A Tribute by Katherine Hepburn" (PBS-TV, 3/22/87).

37. William Gargan's Father Dolan, a prison chaplain in *You Only Live Once* (1937), was such a priest, although much less forceful than those played by Tracy or O'Brien.

38. James Agee, *Agee on Film,* 2 vols. (New York: Universal Library, 1969), 1:347.

39. John Ford to Bing Crosby, February, 1944, Box 1, folder 1944, John Ford Papers, Lilly Library, Indiana University.

40. Schumach, *Face,* 98.

41. The Keysers have a useful, if digressive, discussion of the role of the Irish priest in the 1930s and 1940s; *Hollywood,* 62–76, 94–112.

42. Although perhaps most people were unaware that Brooklyn-born Ruby Stevens was the grandchild on both sides of Irish immigrants. Al DiOrio, *Barbara Stanwyck* (New York: Berkley Books, 1985), 1–2.

43. Physical appearance also disqualified Anthony Quinn, whose mother was Mexican, for Irish roles. Like Naish, Quinn played a variety of other ethnic parts.

44. The virtual disappearance of Jewish subjects from the screen was confirmed in the adaptation of Irwin Shaw's play *The Gentle People* for the movies. In this film, *Out of the Fog* (1941), Thomas Mitchell plays an Irish tailor who was Jewish in the play.

45. Paramount also produced a pedestrian biography of Ireland's most famous composer, *The Great Victor Herbert* (1939), in which the score far outshines the rest of the film.

46. For these two films, see pp. 76–78.

47. For a highly appreciative review of *Beloved Enemy* with the original ending, see that by Frank S. Nugent, *New York Times Film Reviews* 2:1350. For Nugent's negative reaction to the two-endings device, see *New York Times,* January 17, 1937, Section B.

48. Nor should one forget Hibernian "private eyes," such as Michael Shayne (Lloyd Nolan) and Kitty O'Day (Jean Parker) (1940–1942, 1944–1945). Roger Dooley, "The Irish on the Screen: II," *Films in Review* 8

(1957), 259–270, was very helpful in providing references to some of the lesser known movies of the decade.

49. Lawrence J. McCaffrey, *The Irish Diaspora in America* (Bloomington: Indiana University Press, 1976), 96.

CHAPTER 4

1. In a characteristic description of his forebears, Ford wrote his nephew in 1937: "I am glad you [got] the good part of the O'Feeney [sic] blood—some of it is very God-damned awful—we are liars, weaklings & selfish drunkards—but there has always been a stout rebel quality in the family and a peculiar passion for justice. I am glad you inherited the good strain." John Ford to Bob Ford, September ?, 1937, Box 1, folder 1937, John Ford Papers (JFP), Lilly Library, Indiana University.

2. Tag Gallagher, *John Ford: The Man and His Films* (Berkeley: University of California Press, 1986), 2–3. Baptized John Martin Feeney, he took the name Ford from his older brother Francis, who had adopted it early in his acting career.

3. Ford included snatches of Gaelic dialogue in such films as *The Informer, The Quiet Man*, and *The Rising of the Moon*.

4. Ford remarked to a friend that it was only when John F. Kennedy was elected president of the United States in 1960 that he felt like a first-class citizen. James Warner Bellah interview (tape transcript), B. 11, f. 16, JFP. For Ford's background and early years, see Gallagher, *John Ford*, 1–6, Ford's reminiscences (tape transcript) B. 11, f. 29, JFP; Dan Ford, *Pappy: The Life of John Ford* (Englewood Cliffs, N.J.: Prentice-Hall, 1979), 1–10, 233; Andrew Sinclair, *John Ford* (New York: Dial Press/James Wade, 1979), 3–17.

5. Most of Ford's films are set in the past when issues seemed simpler and individuals and situations were easier to dramatize.

6. Peter Bogdanovich, *John Ford*, 2nd ed. (Berkeley: University of California Press, 1978), 59.

7. Ford's reminiscences, B.11, f. 31, JFP.

8. Ford, however, "being Irish" and "a little more sentimental than the average Anglo" ascribed the declining popularity of movies partly to their lack of sentiment. Ford's reminiscences, B.11, f. 31, JFP.

9. For example, James Agee wrote of *Fort Apache* (1948): "there is enough Irish comedy to make me wish Cromwell had done a more thorough job." Agee, 311. Andrew Sarris echoed this complaint about "boisterous Irishness" in *Fort Apache*, adding that from 1948 until the end of his career, "Ford seemed to let everything hang out, and especially his boozy, misty-eyed Irishness." But Sarris also noted that "the broadness of

his humor is the price we must pay for the depth of his feelings." Andrew Sarris, *The John Ford Movie Mystery* (Bloomington: Indiana University Press, 1975), 124, 129, 130.

10. Ford also employed MacDonald as comic relief in his epic *The Iron Horse* (1924). MacDonald plays Corporal Pat Casey, Union Army veteran and tracklayer for both the Union Pacific and Central Pacific Railroads; he steals every scene in which he appears.

11. MOMA has prints of *Shamrock Handicap*, *Riley the Cop*, and *Hangman's House*.

12. Bogdanovich, *John Ford*, 59. Ford later recalled, however, that he still thought *The Informer* was "a great picture" and "a great character study." Ford's reminiscences, B. 11, f. 29, JFP.

13. O'Flaherty's novel dealt with a (largely imaginary) struggle by Irish Communists against the newly established Irish Free State. By contrast, the film is set during the successful rebellion against Britain that produced the Free State. The plot change reflected Ford's militant nationalism and was designed to make the picture more appealing to American audiences. The film's only glaring factual error is its time setting: 1922. The Anglo-Irish war ended in 1921, as Ford well knew, since he was visiting Ireland when the peace treaty was signed in December 1921. Ford's reminiscences, B. 11, f. 29, JFP; John Ford to Mary Ford, December 1921, B. 1, f. 1921, JFP.

14. In addition to Oscars for best direction, actor, script, and score, *The Informer* was named best picture by the New York Film Critics, who also named Ford as best director. On *The Informer*, see Bogdanovich, *John Ford*, 59–64; Dan Ford, *Pappy*, 82–89; Sinclair, *John Ford*, 63–66; Sarris, *John Ford Movie*, 67–70; J. A. Place, *The Non-Western Films of John Ford* (Secaucus, N.J.: Citadel Press, 1979), 152–161.

15. Stanwyck treasured the experience of working with Ford, however, and regretted she never got the chance to do so again. Barbara Stanwyck to John Ford, November 25, 1962, B. 3, f. August-December, 1962, JFP; Robert Blees, "Barbara Stanwyck," *American Film* 12:6 (1987), 42.

16. The studio also added newsreel footage to enhance realism. The footage used, however, is of the civil war of 1922–1923, not the 1916 insurrection. On *The Plough and the Stars*, see Bogdanovich, *John Ford*, 64–66; Place, *Non-Western Films*, 162–168; Blees, "Barbara Stanwyck," 42.

17. Lindsay Anderson, *About John Ford . . .* (New York: McGraw-Hill, 1983), 64–65.

18. Ibid., 22; Place, *Non-Western Films*, 195–196.

19. A feminist could have a field day with this situation, denouncing

the dowry as a barbarous practice while defending Mary Kate's attitude toward it. See, e.g., Molly Haskell, *From Reverence to Rape: The Treatment of Women in the Movies* (New York: Penguin Books, 1979), 269.

20. Ford preferred to work in black-and-white photography but realized that only color could create the mood he wished to convey in this film (Bogdanovich, *John Ford*, 74). Realizing also that violence would destroy this mood, Ford wisely abandoned the idea of setting the story during the "Troubles" of 1920–1921 (Dan Ford, *Pappy*, 241). Absence of a specific time frame helps give the movie its sense of timelessness.

21. On *The Quiet Man*, see Dan Ford, *Pappy*, 240–247; Place, *Non-Western Films*, 195–203; Sarris, *John Ford Movie*, 131–135; Anderson, *About John Ford*, 129–132; Joseph McBride and Michael Wilmington, *John Ford* (New York: Da Capo Press, 1975), 110–124.

22. Bogdanovich, *John Ford*, 30–31.

23. Leaving Ireland after shooting the film's exterior scenes in Connemara, Ford wrote to an Irish friend: "I was all choked up at leaving our beloved Ireland. . . . Galway is in my blood and the only place I have found peace." Sinclair, *John Ford*, 169.

24. Bogdanovich, *John Ford*, 143.

25. Here, as elsewhere in his films, Ford relies heavily on British as well as Irish stereotypes. Despite his Irish nationalism, Ford treated the British with humorous condescension or measured respect rather than hostility, except for the notorious "Black and Tans," who terrorized Ireland in 1920–1921.

26. Whose title, in turn, is taken from a rousing ballad about the bloody uprising of 1798.

27. On *The Rising of the Moon*, see McBride and Wilmington, *John Ford*, 124–134; Place, *Non-Western Films*, 205–208.

28. The score was by the brilliant young composer Sean O'Riada, whose untimely death in 1971 was a tragic loss to the world of music.

29. On *Young Cassidy*, see Bogdanovich, *John Ford*, 106–107; Dan Ford, *Pappy*, 303–305; Place, *Non-Western Films*, 209–219. Robert D. Graff to John Ford, September 9, 1964, and Robert E. Ginna to John Ford, September 9, 1964, B. 3, f. July-September, 1964, JFP.

30. See note 9.

31. Thursday's rejection of the elder O'Rourke's offer to retire from the army and the younger's offer to resign his commission shows that his objection to the marriage is not just a matter of military convention.

32. On *Fort Apache*, see McBride and Wilmington, *John Ford*, 97–109; Sinclair, *John Ford*, 142–145; Gallagher, *John Ford*, 246–254.

33. Dan Ford claims that service in World War II made his grandfather

feel enthusiastic about the military and much less an outsider than he had before the war. In the postwar period, when he selected his own stories, a large number of Ford's movies were about the military, a marked change from his earlier work. Dan Ford interview, "The Moviemakers" (PBS-TV, 11/24/85); see also Dan Ford, *Pappy*, 201, 206–208; Gallagher *John Ford*, 245.

34. On *The Long Gray Line*, see Place, *Non-Western Films*, 121–133; Sarris, *John Ford Movie*, 136–137; Sinclair, *John Ford*, 173–174; Gallagher, *John Ford*, 499.

35. On *The Last Hurrah*, see Bogdanovich, *John Ford*, 91, 96; Place, *Non-Western Films*, 76–81; Sinclair, *John Ford*, 183–184.

36. Bogdanovich, *John Ford*, 75–76.

37. Ford's reminiscences, B. 11, f. 30, JFP.

38. Ibid.

39. Philip Dunne, *Take Two: A Life in Movies and Politics* (New York: McGraw-Hill, 1980), 99.

40. Gallagher, *John Ford*, 341.

41. Cited in McBride and Wilmington, *John Ford*, 37.

CHAPTER 5

1. William V. Shannon, *The American Irish* (New York: Macmillan, 1963), 144.

2. "Wild Bill" Donovan, the 69th's commanding officer, would soon be recalled to active service by President Roosevelt. Having won the Congressional Medal of Honor in World War I, Donovan returned to build a lucrative law practice in New York and became prominent in Republican (!) politics. During World War II, Major General Donovan created and headed the Office of Strategic Services (OSS), which later became the Central Intelligence Agency (CIA). President Eisenhower called Donovan "the last hero," and John Ford, whose Field Photographic Branch was part of the OSS, wanted to film the story of Donovan's work in World War II, with John Wayne in the leading role, but the project was never realized. Tag Gallagher, *John Ford: The Man and His Films* (Berkeley: University of California Press, 1986), 202, 214, 216–217, 545.

3. *New York Times Film Reviews* 3: 1869.

4. James Cagney, *Cagney by Cagney* (New York: Pocket Books, 1977), 119–123; Patrick McGilligan, ed., *Yankee Doodle Dandy* (Madison: University of Wisconsin Press, 1981), 11–64.

5. Tino Balio, ed., *The American Film Industry* (Madison: University of Wisconsin Press, 1976), 222–227.

6. *New York Times Film Reviews* 3:1984. Thomas Mitchell turned

in another sterling performance in 1944 as Joe Tumulty, President Woodrow Wilson's secretary, in Darryl F. Zanuck's grandiose *Wilson*.

7. McCarey's attempt to make the Nazis a laughing matter in *Once Upon a Honeymoon* (1942) was much less successful. However, the "typical American" hero and heroine of the story he co-authored were named Pat O'Toole (Cary Grant) and Katie O'Hara (Ginger Rogers).

8. Richard Polenberg, *One Nation Divisible: Class, Race, and Ethnicity in the United States since 1938* (New York: Viking Press, 1980), 60–61.

9. Patrick J. Blessing, "The Irish," *Harvard Encyclopedia of American Ethnic Groups,* ed. Stephen Thernstrom (Cambridge, Mass.: The Belknap Press, 1980), 541–543; James Hennesey, *American Catholics: A History of the Roman Catholic Community in the United States* (New York: Oxford University Press, 1981), 283.

10. Balio, *American Film,* 315–320; Garth Jowett, *Film: The Democratic Art* (Boston: Little, Brown, 1976), 473, 475.

11. Balio, *American Film,* 318–320; Murray Schumach, *The Face on the Cutting Room Floor* (New York: William Morrow, 1964), 88–89.

12. Balio, *American Film,* 320–325.

13. Ibid., 328.

14. Ibid., 326–328; Jack C. Ellis, *A History of Film* (Englewood Cliffs, N.J.: Prentice-Hall, 1979), 256–261; Victor S. Navasky, *Naming Names* (New York: Penguin Books, 1980), *passim.*

15. Thomas J. Archdeacon, *Becoming American: An Ethnic History* (New York: The Free Press, 1983), 199–201; Blessing, "The Irish," 543; Hennesey, *American Catholics,* 292–295; Polenberg, *One Nation,* 126; John Cogley, *Catholic America* (New York: The Dial Press, 1973), 111–114; Nathan Glazer and Daniel Patrick Moynihan, *Beyond the Melting Pot: The Negroes, Puerto Ricans, Jews, Italians, and Irish of New York City* (Cambridge, Mass.: MIT Press and Harvard University Press, 1963), 269–271.

16. Glazer and Moynihan, *Beyond,* 270.

17. Ibid., 271.

18. Navasky, *Naming,* 177, 180–181; Philip Dunne, *Take Two: A Life in Movies and Politics* (New York: McGraw-Hill, 1980), 119–120, 196, 199, 268; Gallagher, *John Ford,* 339-341; Larry Ceplair and Steven Englund, *The Inquisition in Hollywood: Politics in the Film Community, 1930–1960* (New York: Doubleday, 1980), *passim;* Garry Wills, *Reagan's America: Innocents at Home* (New York: Doubleday, 1987), 241–258. Regarding Ford, except for his enthusiastic Americanism, he was basically apolitical, describing himself at various times in his career as "a definite socialist Democrat," "a fervent, lifelong Democrat," and "a rock-

ribbed Republican." He was also an ardent admirer of FDR, Eisenhower, John F. Kennedy, and Richard Nixon. Responding to his Irish and Democratic heritage, as well as to the popular mood, Ford supported the New Deal in the 1930s. Wartime naval service intensified his devotion to traditional institutions, especially the armed services, and postwar developments made him, like many other Americans, increasingly conservative. However, Ford never became a right-wing ideologue, like his close friend John Wayne.

19. *New York Times Film Reviews* 4: 2603.

20. Peter Roffman and Jim Purdy, *The Hollywood Social Problem Film: Madness, Despair, and Politics from the Depression to the Fifties* (Bloomington: Indiana University Press, 1981), 290–293; Polenberg, *One Nation,* 96; Ellis, *History,* 257; Stefan Kanfer, *A Journal of the Plague Years* (New York: Atheneum, 1973), 189–192. Political conservative John Lee Mahin wrote the original script for *My Son John,* but he downplayed the anti-Communist theme of McCarey's story, fearing the sermonizing would bore the audience. To Mahin's dismay, and that of Helen Hayes who had agreed to do the picture on the basis of Mahin's script, McCarey rewrote the screenplay, making it an anti-Communist diatribe. Both Mahin and liberal screenwriter Donald Ogden Stewart, who had worked with McCarey on an earlier film, agree that McCarey's anti-Communism was an obsession, something that Stewart attributed to his Catholicism. Pat McGilligan, ed., *Backstory: Interviews with Screenwriters of Hollywood's Golden Age* (Berkeley: University of California Press, 1986), 261, 247. Congratulating John Ford on the success of his recent film, McCarey wrote: "The Quiet Man is going great—I'm glad Mrs. O'Fearna's [sic] son John is doing better than 'My Son John.' " Apparently, McCarey could not resist adding: "The other night at an SDG [Screen Directors Guild] meeting we attached a lie detector to a well-known member—When he said he'd never been a Commie—the fuse blew out!" Leo McCarey to John Ford, B. 2, f. December 1953, JFP. This memo has no date, but it was probably written in 1952 rather than 1953.

21. The fact that it is an Irishman who breaks the code of silence and turns in "his own people" to the authorities underlines the film's message that, in certain circumstances, informing is a moral duty rather than a heinous sin.

22. Kenneth R. Hey, "On the Waterfront," *American Quarterly* 31 (1979), 666–696; Navasky, *Naming,* 199–222, 239–246.

23. On Gene Kelly and postwar America, see Michael Wood, *America at the Movies* (New York: Delta Books, 1975), 146–164.

CHAPTER 6

1. Norman Yetman, "The Irish Experience in America," *Irish History and Culture: Aspects of a People's Heritage,* ed. Harold Orel (Lawrence: University Press of Kansas, 1976), 372.

2. Patrick J. Blessing, "The Irish," *Harvard Encyclopedia of American Ethnic Groups,* ed. Stephen Thernstrom (Cambridge, Mass.: The Belknap Press, 1980), 543.

3. Andrew M. Greeley, *The Irish Americans: The Rise to Money and Power* (New York: Harper and Row, 1981), 1–3, 9, 108, 111, 148–149, 167–168, 199–207; Marjorie R. Fallows, *Irish Americans: Identity and Assimilation* (Englewood Cliffs, N.J.: Prentice-Hall, 1979), 60–80, 143–149; Thomas J. Archdeacon, *Becoming American: An Ethnic History* (New York: The Free Press, 1983), 224–229; Yetman, "Irish Experience," 362–364, 369–372.

4. Tino Balio, ed., *The American Film Industry* (Madison: University of Wisconsin Press, 1976), 329–331; *New York Times,* May 31, 1987, Sect. 3, p. 1.

5. Ephraim Katz, *The Film Encyclopedia* (New York: Perigee Books, 1979), 707–708, 934, 949; Charles Champlin, "What Will Hays Begot," *American Film* 6.1. (1980), 42–46, 86–88.

6. William V. Shannon, *The American Irish* (New York: Macmillan, 1963), 278.

7. Ibid., 276.

8. For an extended discussion of *Goodbar,* see Les and Barbara Keyser, *Hollywood and the Catholic Church: The Image of Roman Catholicism in American Movies* (Chicago: Loyola University Press, 1984), 258–264.

9. This favorable presentation was undoubtedly a product of the civil rights upheaval of the 1960s. As miners with blackened faces are forced to resort to violence to secure social justice for an oppressed ethnic minority, so militant blacks are justified in using violence to secure their legitimate ends. Ritt and Bernstein's interpretation shows how present-mindedness can distort the depiction of historical reality. The best study of the Mollies is Wayne Broehl, *The Molly Maguires* (Cambridge: Harvard University Press, 1964).

10. "Dialogue on Film: Martin Ritt," *American Film* 9.2 (1983), 22.

11. Irish-American Patty Duke also won an Oscar, as best supporting actress, for her performance as Helen Keller.

12. Richard Polenberg, *One Nation Divisible: Class, Race, and Ethnicity in the United States Since 1938* (New York: Viking Press, 1980), 224–225.

13. The hostility of some Jewish filmmakers toward the Irish and what they are perceived to represent is shown in *The Heartbreak Kid* (1972). In it, the Jewish hero's dreamgirl is an "Irish princess" named Kelly Corcoran. To pursue this elusive blond goddess, the hero abandons his Jewish bride on their honeymoon. To win her, he gives up not only his bride, but also his family, friends, ethnic heritage, and any chance he might have had at lasting happiness. In contending that Jews who accept the mainstream cultural values represented by the Irish must thereby betray their own heritage, much as the Corcorans, who are colorless WASPs in all but name, have betrayed theirs, *The Heartbreak Kid* rejects the assimilationist thesis popularized by films of the *Abie's Irish Rose* school. Just because the Irish have allegedly "sold out" to the establishment is no reason for the Jews to do so. On this film, see Lester D. Friedman, *Hollywood's Image of the Jew* (New York: Frederick Ungar, 1982), 253–256.

14. Fallows, *Irish Americans*, 61.

15. Lawrence J. McCaffrey, *The Irish Diaspora in America* (Bloomington: Indiana University Press, 1976), 176.

16. In addition to the obvious changes in speech, dress, behavior, neighborhood, income, education, and occupation, Irish attitudes toward religion, race, sex, family size, and ethnic intermarriage have changed markedly, especially in the past quarter century or so.

☆ ☆ ☆

Selected Bibliography

FILM ARCHIVES

The Library of Congress, Washington, D.C.
> Motion Picture, Broadcasting and Recorded Sound Division (silent films)

Museum of Modern Art, New York City
> Film Study Center (silent films)

Wisconsin Center for Film and Theater Research, Madison, Wisconsin
> Film and Manuscript Archives (Warner Bros. films of the 1930s and 1940s)

PRIVATE PAPERS

John Ford Papers, Manuscripts Department, Lilly Library, Indiana University, Bloomington, Indiana

BOOKS AND ARTICLES

Agee, James. *Agee on Film,* Vol. 1. New York: Universal Library, 1969.

Amberg, George, ed. *New York Times Film Reviews, 1913–1968,* 6 vols. New York: Arno Press, 1971.

Anderson, Lindsay. *About John Ford.* . . . New York: McGraw-Hill, 1983.

Archdeacon, Thomas J. *Becoming American: An Ethnic History.* New York: The Free Press, 1983.

Balio, Tino, ed. *The American Film Industry*. Madison: University of Wisconsin Press, 1976.

Behlmer, Rudy. *Inside Warner Brothers (1935–1951)*. New York: Viking Penguin, 1985.

Bergman, Andrew. *We're in the Money: Depression America and Its Films*. New York: New York University Press, 1971.

Blessing, Patrick J. "The Irish." *Harvard Encyclopedia of American Ethnic Groups*. Ed Stephen Thernstrom, 524–545. Cambridge, Mass.: The Belknap Press, 1980.

Bogdanovich, Peter. *John Ford*, rev. ed. Berkeley: University of California Press, 1978.

Brown, Thomas N. *Irish-American Nationalism, 1870–1890*. Philadelphia: J. B. Lippicott, 1966.

Brownlow, Kevin. *The Parade's Gone By*. Berkeley: University of California Press, 1968.

Cagney, James. *Cagney by Cagney*. New York: Pocket Books, 1977.

Ceplair, Larry and Steven Englund. *The Inquisition in Hollywood: Politics in the Film Community, 1930–1960*. New York: Doubleday, 1980.

Cogley, John. *Catholic America*. New York: The Dial Press, 1973.

Cohen, Henry, ed. *The Public Enemy*. Madison: University of Wisconsin Press, 1981.

Cross, Robert D. "The Irish." *Ethnic Leadership in America*. Ed. John Higham, 176–197. Baltimore: The Johns Hopkins University Press, 1978.

Current Biography. New York: H. H. Wilson Company, 1940–.

Curtis, Jr. L.P. *Anglo-Saxons and Celts: A Study of Anti-Irish Prejudice in Victorian England*. Bridgeport, Conn.: Conference on British Studies, 1968.

Donovan, Kathleen. "Good Old Pat: An Irish-American Stereotype in Decline." *Eire-Ireland* 15.3 (1980): 6–14.

Dooley, Roger B. "The Irish on the Screen: I and II." *Films in Review*, 8.5 and 6 (1957): 211–217 and 259–270.

Dunne, Philip. *Take Two: A Life in Movies and Politics*. New York: McGraw-Hill, 1980.

Ellis, Jack C. *A History of Film*. Englewood Cliffs, N.J.: Prentice-Hall, 1979.

Erens, Patricia. *The Jew in American Cinema*. Bloomington: Indiana University Press, 1984.

Fallows, Marjorie R. *Irish Americans: Identity and Assimilation*. Englewood Cliffs, N.J.: Prentice-Hall, 1979.

Fanning, Charles. "Mr. Dooley in Chicago: Finley Peter Dunne as Historian of the Irish in America." *America and Ireland, 1776–1976: The American Identity and the Irish Connection*. Eds. David Noel Doyle and Owen Dudley Edwards, 151–163. Westport, Conn.: Greenwood Press, 1980.

Feagin, Joe R. *Racial and Ethnic Relations*. Englewood Cliffs, N.J.: Prentice-Hall, 1978.

Fielder, Mari Kathleen. "Fatal Attraction: Irish-Jewish Romance in Early Film and Drama." *Eire-Ireland*, 20.3 (1985): 6–18.

Ford, Dan. *Pappy: The Life of John Ford*. Englewood Cliffs, N.J.: Prentice-Hall, 1979.

Friedman, Lester D. *Hollywood's Image of the Jew*. New York: Frederick Ungar, 1982.

Gallagher, Tag. *John Ford: The Man and His Films*. Berkeley: University of California Press, 1986.

Glazer, Nathan and Daniel Patrick Moynihan. *Beyond the Melting Pot: The Negroes, Puerto Ricans, Jews, Italians, and Irish of New York City*. Cambridge, Mass.: The MIT Press and Harvard University Press, 1963.

Gleason, Philip. "American Identity and Americanization." *Harvard Encyclopedia of American Ethnic Groups*. Ed. Stephen Thernstrom, 31–58. Cambridge, Mass.: The Belknap Press, 1980.

Gomery, Douglas. *The Hollywood Studio System*. London: Macmillan, 1986.

Greeley, Andrew M. *The Irish Americans: The Rise to Money and Power*. New York: Harper and Row, 1981.

Hampton, Benjamin B. *History of the American Film Industry from its Beginnings to 1931*. New York: Dover Publications, 1970 (1931).

Helmreich, William B. *The Things They Say Behind Your Back*. New York: Doubleday, 1982.

Hennesey, James. *American Catholics: A History of the Roman Catholic Community in the United States*. New York: Oxford University Press, 1981.

Higham, John. *Strangers in the Land: Patterns of American Nativism, 1860–1925*. New York: Atheneum, 1969.

Jacobs, Lewis. *The Rise of the American Film: A Critical History*. New York: Columbia University, 1968 (1939).

Jones, Maldwyn A. "The Scotch-Irish." *Harvard Encyclopedia of American Ethnic Groups*. Ed. Stephen Thernstrom, 895–908. Cambridge, Mass.: The Belknap Press, 1980.

Jowett, Garth. *Film: The Democratic Art*. Boston: Little, Brown, 1976.

Kahn, Jr., E. J. *The Merry Partners: The Age and Stage of Harrigan and Hart*. New York: Random House, 1955.

Kanfer, Stefan. *A Journal of the Plague Years*. New York: Atheneum, 1973.

Kanin, Garson. *Tracy and Hepburn: An Intimate Memoir*. New York: Viking Press, 1971.

Katz, Ephraim. *The Film Encyclopedia*. New York: Perigee Books, 1979.

Keyser, Les and Barbara. *Hollywood and the Catholic Church: The Image of Roman Catholicism in American Movies*. Chicago: Loyola University Press, 1984.

Kirstein, Lincoln. "James Cagney and the American Hero." *American Film Criticism: From the Beginnings to Citizen Kane*. Ed. Stanley Kauffmann, with Bruce Henstell, 262–264. New York: Liveright, 1972.

Kobal, John. *People Will Talk*. New York: Alfred A. Knopf, 1985.

Krafsur, Richard P., ed. *The American Film Institute Catalog of Motion Pictures Produced in the United States: Feature Films, 1961–70.* New York: Bowker, 1976.

Larkin, Emmet. *The Historical Dimensions of Irish Catholicism*. Washington, D.C.: Catholic University of America Press, 1984.

Lord, Daniel A., S.J. *Played by Ear: The Autobiography of Daniel A. Lord, S.J.* Chicago: Loyola University Press, 1956.

McAvoy, Thomas T., C.S.C. *A History of the Catholic Church in the United States*. Notre Dame, Ind.: University of Notre Dame Press, 1969.

McBride, Joseph, and Michael Wilmington. *John Ford*. New York: Da Capo Press, 1975.

McCaffrey, Lawrence J. *The Irish Diaspora in America*. Bloomington: Indiana University Press, 1976.

McClure, Arthur F. "Censor the Movies! Early Attempts to Regulate the Content of Motion Pictures in America, 1907–1936." *The Movies: An American Idiom—Readings in the Social History of the American Motion Picture*. Ed. Arthur F. McClure, 117–152. Rutherford, N.J.: Fairleigh Dickinson Press, 1971.

McGilligan, Patrick. *Cagney: The Actor as Auteur*, rev. ed. San Diego: A. S. Barnes, 1982 (1975).

McGilligan, Patrick, ed. *Backstory: Interviews with Screenwriters of Hollywood's Golden Age*. Berkeley: University of California Press, 1986.

McGilligan, Patrick, ed. *Yankee Doodle Dandy*. Madison: University of Wisconsin Press, 1981.

MacGowan, Kenneth. *Behind the Screen: The History and Techniques of the Motion Picture*. New York: Delacorte Press, 1965.

McLean, Jr., Albert F. *American Vaudeville as Ritual*. Lexington: University of Kentucky Press, 1965.

Maltby, Richard. *Harmless Entertainment: Hollywood and the Ideology of Consensus*. Metuchen, N.J.: Scarecrow Press, 1983.

May, Lary. *Screening Out the Past: The Birth of Mass Culture and the Motion Picture Industry*. New York: Oxford University Press, 1980.

Miller, Kerby A. *Emigrants and Exiles: Ireland and the Irish Exodus to North America*. New York: Oxford University Press, 1985.

Miller, Randall M., ed. *The Kaleidoscopic Lens: How Hollywood Views Ethnic Groups*. n.p.: Jerome S. Ozer, 1980.

Mitchell, George. "Sidney Olcott." *Films in Review*, 5.4 (1954): 175–181.

Mitchell, George J. "Ford on Ford." *Films in Review*, 15.6 (1964): 321–332.

Moley, Raymond. *The Hays Office*. Indianapolis: Bobbs-Merrill, 1945.

Munden, Kenneth W., ed. *The American Film Institute Catalog of Motion Pictures Produced in the United States: Feature Films, 1921–30*. New York: Bowker, 1971.

Murphy, Maureen. "Irish-American Theatre." *Ethnic Theatre in the United States*. Ed. Maxine Schwartz Seller, 221–235. Westport, Conn.: Greenwood Press, 1983.

Navasky, Victor S. *Naming Names*. New York: Penguin Books, 1980.

Niver, Kemp R. *Motion Pictures from the Library of Congress Paper Print Collection, 1894–1912*. Berkeley: University of California Press, 1967.

O'Brien, Pat. *The Wind at My Back: The Life and Times of Pat O'Brien*. New York: Doubleday, 1964.

Parrish, Robert. *Growing Up in Hollywood*. New York: Harcourt Brace Jovanovich, 1976.

Place, J. A. *The Non-Western Films of John Ford*. Secaucus, N.J.: Citadel Press, 1979.

Polenberg, Richard. *One Nation Divisible: Class, Race, and Ethnicity in the United States Since 1938*. New York: Viking Press, 1980.

Potter, George. *To the Golden Door: The Story of the Irish in Ireland and America*. Boston: Little, Brown, 1960.

Powdermaker, Hortense. *Hollywood: The Dream Factory*. Boston: Little, Brown, 1951.

Ramsaye, Terry. *A Million and One Nights: A History of the Motion Picture*, Vol. 2. New York: Simon and Schuster, 1926.

Randall, Richard S. *Censorship of the Movies: The Social and Political Control of a Mass Medium*. Madison: University of Wisconsin Press, 1968.

Reagan, Ronald, with Richard G. Hubler. *Where's the Rest of Me?* New York: Duell, Sloan, and Pearce, 1965.

Roddick, Nick. *A New Deal in Entertainment: Warner Brothers in the 1930s*. London: British Film Institute, 1983.

Roffman, Peter and Jim Purdy. *The Hollywood Social Problem Film:*

Madness, Despair, and Politics from the Depression to the Fifties. Bloomington: Indiana University Press, 1981.

Rosten, Leo C. *Hollywood: The Movie Colony, The Movie Makers.* New York: Harcourt, Brace and Company, 1941.

Russell, Rosalind, and Chris Chase. *Life is a Banquet.* New York: Random House, 1977.

Sarris, Andrew. *The John Ford Movie Mystery.* Bloomington: Indiana University Press, 1975.

Schatz, Thomas. *Hollywood Genres: Formulas, Filmmaking, and the Studio System.* Austin: University of Texas, 1981.

Schumach, Murray. *The Face on the Cutting Room Floor.* New York: William Morrow, 1964.

Sennett, Ted. *Warner Brothers Presents.* New Rochelle, N.Y.: Arlington House, 1971.

Shannon, William V. *The American Irish.* New York: Macmillan, 1963.

Sinclair, Andrew. *John Ford.* New York: The Dial Press/James Wade, 1979.

Sklar, Robert. *Movie-Made America: A Cultural History of American Movies.* New York: Vintage Books, 1975.

Sowell, Thomas. *Ethnic America: A History.* New York: Basic Books, 1981.

Stivers, Richard. *A Hair of the Dog: Irish Drinking and American Stereotype.* University Park: Pennsylvania State University Press, 1976.

Swindell, Larry. *Spencer Tracy . . . A Biography.* New York: World, 1969.

Thorp, Margaret. *America at the Movies.* New Haven, Conn.: Yale University Press, 1939.

Tynan, Kenneth. *Curtains.* New York: Atheneum, 1961.

U.S. Bureau of the Census. *Statistical Abstract of the United States: 1985.* Washington, D.C., 1984.

Vizzard, Jack. *See No Evil: Life Inside a Hollywood Censor.* New York: Simon and Schuster, 1970.

Wallis, Hal and Charles Higham. *Starmaker: The Autobiography of Hal Wallis.* New York: Macmillan, 1980.

Walsh, Raoul. *Each Man in His Time.* New York: Farrar, Straus, and Giroux, 1974.

Warner, Jack L., with Dean Jennings. *My First Hundred Years in Hollywood.* New York: Random House, 1965.

Warren, Doug, with James Cagney. *James Cagney: The Authorized Biography.* New York: St. Martin's Press, 1983.

Whalen, Richard J. *The Founding Father: The Story of Joseph P. Kennedy.* New York: New American Library, 1964.

Wills, Gary. *Reagan's America: Innocents at Home*. New York: Doubleday, 1987.

Wilson, Robert, ed. *The Film Criticism of Otis Ferguson*. Philadelphia: Temple University Press, 1971.

Wittke, Carl. *The Irish in America*. Baton Rouge: Louisiana State University Press, 1956.

Wood, Michael. *America in the Movies*. New York: Delta Books, 1975.

Yetman, Norman. "The Irish Experience in America." *Irish History and Culture: Aspects of a People's Heritage*. Ed. Harold Orel, 347–376. Lawrence: The University Press of Kansas, 1976.

☆ ☆ ☆

Index

About the Author

JOSEPH M. CURRAN is a Professor of History at Le Moyne College in Syracuse, New York. He is the author of *The Birth of the Irish Free State, 1921–1923,* and has published articles in *Historian, Irish University Review* (Dublin), and *America.*

BEVERLY BRANCH